Sales and Statistical Forecasting Combined:
Mixing Approaches for Improved Forecast Accuracy

Shaun
Snapp

Contents

CHAPTER 1

Introduction

Statistical forecasting and sales forecasting are two very different ways of arriving at a prediction of future demand. How these two predictors are combined is very important, and in fact is one of the most significant factors in forecast accuracy for any company. Combining statistical and sales forecasting in such a way that an accurate forecast is created requires a stringent process based upon a combination of experience and testing.

This book is focused on putting together the pieces in order to create the most effective forecast. Through the testing described in this book, the optimum combination of statistical and sales forecasting can be determined for each PLC (product-location combination, also known as SKU-L). Many companies have the mistaken belief that they do not require structured testing or a blue-print for how to make the most of the two forecasting approaches. This book provides both the methodology for structured testing and the blueprint, and if the steps are followed, the maximum forecast accuracy can be extracted from the combination of statistical and sales forecasting inputs.

Companies with a High Forecast Error Face Reduced Efficiencies

A high forecast error is quite destructive to a company's internal efficiency. Forecasting environments work most efficiently when everyone knows who is responsible for what and is confident that what can be done is being done. Companies that have problems forecasting end up with all types of inefficien-cies. And the less the forecast is trusted, the more second-guessing takes place or reforecasting is performed—not only within the groups that are ostensibly tasked with forecasting, but in downstream groups as well, such as supply and production planning. At a number of my previous clients, prompted by high forecast inaccuracy, Supply Planning reviews the forecast and then ad-justs things like coverage profiles depending on what **they think** the forecast should be. In these environments, often Production will not produce to the forecast, but produce to what **they think** is most likely to sell. These are both examples of what is referred to as **second guessing**.

In my experience, when the accuracy of a system-generated forecast is known to be low, the justification for altering the forecast is greater, and the lower the forecast error the more compelled those that provide domain expertise to the forecast feel compelled to change the statistical forecast. In interviews with a variety of companies, it is frequently communicated that individuals outside of forecasting will evaluate the forecast to see if it "makes sense"; often they don't believe the forecast and so they make their own adjustments, for instance to supply planning control parameters. This alternate type of forecast adjust-ment is symptomatic within companies where forecast accuracy is low, or is perceived to be low.[1] This is problematic and results in "too many cooks in the kitchen," and can inspire even more groups to make adjustments once they learn that other groups are making adjustments to counteract their adjustments. This is a natural reaction to a poor quality forecast. When the forecast accuracy improves, this second-guessing can undermine the improvement because the degree of second guessing becomes habitual, and those downstream of the forecasting process will continue to make adjustments based upon their historical experience.

Second guessing is highly inefficient. Second guessing means rework, and these downstream groups do not have the systems that a centralized department has to create a forecast, and do not have enough time to allocate to second guessing to ensure a proper job is performed. The end result, typically, is that judgment methods in these areas are applied. It also means that the official forecast is not actually the predominantly factor driving the plan.

Books and Other Publications on Statistical and Sales Forecasting

As with all my books, I performed a comprehensive literature review before I began writing this book. One of my favorite quotations about research is from the highly respected RAND Corporation, a "think tank" based in sunny Santa Monica, CA. They are located not far from where I grew up. On my lost surfing weekends during high school, I used to walk right by their offices with my friend—at that time having no idea of the institution's historical significance. RAND's *Standards for High Quality Research and Analysis* publication makes the following statement about how its research references other work.

> *"A high-quality study cannot be done in intellectual isolation:*
> *It necessarily builds on and contributes to a body of research*
> *and analysis. The relationships between a given study and*

---

[1] Many companies are running a very expensive forecasting process. This is because the low accuracy of the forecast causes so many people to have to make adjustments. This was obvious just from those that I interviewed, and I have not yet spoken to people in manufacturing; however, the forecast accuracy level is imposing negative externalities upon manufacturing productivity.

its predecessors should be rich and explicit. The study team's understanding of past research should be evident in many aspects of its work, from the way in which the problem is formulated and approached to the discussion of the findings and their implications. The team should take particular care to explain the ways in which its study agrees, disagrees, or otherwise differs importantly from previous studies. Failure to demonstrate an understanding of previous research lowers the perceived quality of a study, despite any other good characteristics it may possess."

One of the reasons I was motivated to write this book is that no other book really spends much time explaining specifically how to combine statistical forecasting with sales forecasting. There are good books on statistical forecasting and good books on sales forecasting, but I was unable to find a book that explains the best way to combine these two forecasting streams. In particular, the book *Sales Forecasting Management*, by Mentzer & Bienstock made a large impression on me due to its accuracy, and you will see that I use several quotations from that book. *Sales Forecasting Management* does an excellent job of explaining the common issues that prevent effective sales forecasting. Interestingly, although this book was written in 1998, the book brings up issues that continue to plague companies today. In fact, it is striking, given all the investments in technology, how little has changed since the book was written.

In reality, both statistical and sales forecasting are important and add value, and they must be combined in order to get the best outcomes. However, the explanations of **exactly how to do** this are lacking. This book fills the gap and explains an approach that is both logical and "battle tested" on real forecast improvement projects. After reading this book, I want readers to know exactly what they need to do to combine these two forecasting streams.

Many books on forecasting—particularly books on statistical forecasting—tend to be "ingredient books." That is, they describe and explain all of the tools that are available to produce a forecast. However, they are not cookbooks, in that they don't really tell you how to combine the tools to obtain the desired outcomes. This book is more of a cookbook: it explains how to blend the ingredients into a cohesive whole, and this blended involves the combination of statistical forecasting and sales forecasting.

The approach outlined in this book was not learned from a book or a conference or an academic paper, but was developed and honed through successive forecasting improvement projects. Everything in the book is real and is imbued by actual experiences in businesses as part of my consulting work. If a method is described in this book, I deployed it at some point. In the examples shown throughout the book, techniques used at previous customer sites are explained; only "the names have been changed to protect the innocent."

The Use of Screen Shots in the Book

I consult in some popular and well-known applications, and I've found that companies have often been given the wrong impression of an application's capabilities. As part of my consulting work, I am required to present the results of testing and research about various applications. The research may show that a well-known application is not able to perform some functionality well enough to be used by a company, and point to a lesser-known application where this functionality is easily performed. Because I am routinely in this situation, I am asked to provide evidence of the testing results within applications, and screen shots provide this necessary evidence.

Furthermore, some time ago it became a habit for me to include extensive screen shots in most of my project documentation. A screen shot does not, of course, guarantee that a particular functionality works, but it is the best that can be done in a document format. Everything in this book exists in one application or another, and nothing described in this book is hypothetical.

Timing Field Definitions Identification

This book is filled with lists. Some of these lists are field definitions. The way to quickly identify which lists are field definitions, they will be all *italics*, while lists that are not field definitions will be only *italics* for the term defined, while the definition that follows is not in normal text.

How Writing Bias Is Controlled at SCM Focus and SCM Focus Press

Bias is a serious problem in the enterprise software field. Large vendors receive uncritical coverage of their products, and large consulting companies recommend the large vendors that have the resources to hire and pay consultants rather than the vendors with the best software for the client's needs.

At SCM Focus, we have yet to financially benefit from a company's decision to buy an application showcased in print, either in a book or on the SCM Focus website. This may change in the future as SCM Focus grows – but we have been writing with a strong viewpoint for years without coming into any conflicts of interest. SCM Focus has the most stringent rules related to controlling bias and restricting commercial influence of any information provider. These "writing rules" are provided in the link below:

http://www.scmfocus.com/writing-rules/

If other information providers followed these rules, we would be able to learn about software without being required to perform our own research and testing for every topic.

Information about enterprise supply chain planning software can be found on the Internet, but this information is primarily promotional or written at such a high level that none of the important details or limitations of the application are exposed; this is true of books as well. When only one enterprise software application is covered in a book, one will find that the application works perfectly; the application operates as expected and there are no problems during the implementation to bring the application live. This is all quite amazing and quite different from my experience of implementing enterprise software. However, it is very difficult to make a living by providing objective information about enterprise supply chain software, especially as it means being critical at some point. I once remarked to a friend that SCM Focus had very little competition in providing untarnished information on this software category, and he said, "Of course, there is no money in it."

Important Terminology The Approach to the Book

By writing this book, I wanted to help people get exactly the information they need without having to read a lengthy volume. The approach to the book is essentially the same as to my previous books, and in writing this book I followed the same principles.

1. **Be direct and concise.** There is very little theory in this book and the math that I cover is simple. While the mathematics behind the optimization meth-

ods for supply and production planning is involved, there are plenty of books, which cover this topic. This book is focused on software and for most users and implementers of the software the most important thing to understand is conceptually what the software is doing.

2. **Based on project experience.** Nothing in the book is hypothetical; I have worked with it or tested it on an actual project. My project experience has led to my understanding a number of things that are not covered in typical supply planning books. In this book, I pass on this understanding to you.

3. **Saturate the book with graphics.** Roughly two-thirds of a human's sensory input is visual, and books that do not use graphics—especially educational and training books such as this one—can fall short of their purpose. Graphics have also been used consistently and extensively on the SCM Focus website.

Before writing this book, I spent some time reviewing what has already been published on the subject. This book is different from other books in terms of its intended audience and its scope. It is directed toward people that have either worked with ERP or know what it is; I am assuming that the reader has a basic knowledge level in this area.

To fully understand and benefit from this book, it is necessary to understand the variety of terminology used throughout it. These terms are divided into different categories, which are described below: General Terms, Forecasting Terms, Marketing Terms, Application Terms, and Forecasting Application Fields/Terms.

General Terms

1. *Sales/Marketing:* Refers to any person who is from the Sales or Marketing side of a company.

2. *Supply Chain:* Refers to the Supply Chain department within a company.

3. *Market Intelligence*: This term has a very general definition, but for the

purposes of this book we will only discuss the domain expertise of Sales/ Marketing. This is the combined knowledge of the marketplace, customers, products, etc., that resides with Sales/Marketing and which they use to perform forecast adjustments.

Forecasting Terms

1. *PLC:* The product-location combination. Product A at Location B is one product- location combination.

2. *Attribute-based Forecasting:* This is the ability to assign PLCs to flexible hierarchies for use in the forecasting system. An attribute is any characteristic of the product or location. Attributes can be used for forecasting functionality (such as top-down forecasting), or they can be navigational and used to efficiently segment the PLC database. Attribute-based forecasting is its own topic, and while attribute-based forecasting is similar conceptually across various applications, its implementation within applications differs greatly. Secondly, the quality of the actual attribute capabilities of various forecasting applications that claim the functionality varies. I do not cover attribute-based forecasting in this book from a foundational perspective, but I do explain the importance of attributes for promotions forecasting in the application examples. However, my first forecasting book, *Supply Chain Forecasting Software,* covers attribute-based forecasting extensively.

3. *Forecast-ability:* This is an approximate term used to describe the general maximum forecast accuracy that can be expected from statistically forecasting a PLC. The less forecast-able a PLC, the less any statistical method can add value by creating a forecast. Forecast-ability is important in measuring the performance of any forecasting system/approach/ method, because it places forecast performance within the context of what was hypothetically possible. Forecast-ability addresses the problem of using just the forecast error to determine forecast success or forecast failure. High forecast accuracy does not necessarily validate a method because the item forecasted may be simply easy to forecast. Similarly, low forecast accuracy does not necessarily repudiate a forecasting system/approach/method, because the item may be very difficult to forecast.

4. *Best-fit Procedure:* This is an automated matching of a PLC to the best forecasting method available in the application that is running the procedure. Best fit works on the basis of the history of the PLC.

5. *Stockpiling:* Stockpiling is a general term, which often means to procure items significantly in advance of their usage for a variety of reasons – such as in preparation for a lengthy ocean voyage. However, in this book we will be analyzing the more specialized meaning of the term, which is the purchasing of product ahead of actual consumption in response to an incentive such as a promotion.

6. *Overfitting:* There are at least two ways of defining overfitting, both of which are quite interesting. The practical definition of overfitting is when a model or person creates a forecast model that, while good at matching the history of the predicted item, does not work nearly as well in predicting the future. Wikipedia offers a nice definition that is more technical. I don't think I can improve upon this definition and so I have included it here.[2]

7. *(PAC) Promotion Adjustment Calculator:* A tool for consistently adjusting promotions to the forecast by product category based upon history.

8. *Outlier*: An outlier is a data point that diverges from the other observations of which it is a group. Identification of outliers is one of the steps in accounting for promotions.

9. *Forecasting Lead*: This is a term I use throughout the book. The Forecasting Lead works out of Supply Chain, but works with Sales/Marketing and controls how market intelligence is converted into inputs for Sales/Marketing forecasts, as well as manages the statistical forecast. Depend-

---

[2] *"Overfitting generally occurs when a model is excessively complex, such as having too many parameters relative to the number of observations. A model which has been overfit will generally have poor predictive performance, as it can exaggerate minor fluctuations in the data. The possibility of overfitting exists because the criterion used for training the model is not the same as the criterion used to judge the efficacy of a model. In particular, a model is typically trained by maximizing its performance on some set of training data. However, its efficacy is determined not by its performance on the training data but by its ability to perform well on unseen data. Overfitting occurs when a model begins to memorize training data rather than learning to generalize from trend." -* Wikipedia

ing upon the company size, this "role" may actually be several people. Or there may be several people that support the Forecasting Lead, typically doing more of the technical work. I don't want to spend time describing the exact configuration of the Forecasting Lead because it depends upon the particular company, so in this case one size does not fit all. The Forecasting Lead position is a highly communicative position, and it is the linchpin or conduit between Sales/Marketing and Supply Chain.

10. *Second Guessing*: This occurs when the statistical and or the sales forecast delivers a high forecast error. It results in adjustments being made in downstream planning, and of decentralizing the forecasting activity from the Forecasting department to other groups within the company, such as Supply Planning and Production Planning. While multiple forecasts are produced as a result, these downstream adjustments are not officially forecasts.

Application Terms

I will be using screen shots of a forecasting application to illustrate different observations from testing, so let's go over an explanation of what you will view in these screen shots.

1. *Resultant History:* This is the black line in the user interface of Demand Works Smoothie, the primary application used in this book to explain promotions. The Resultant History is the actual sales history plus any adjustments. It is not the Actual History.

2. *Fitted Forecast*: The red line you will see in the user interface screen shots is the Fitted Forecast. This is the forecast of the model in the past. Many of those who work in forecasting refer to this as the "ex-post" forecast. However, I don't use this term myself because its jargon and not helpful in explaining what it describes. But I include it here just in case others who read this book do use the term. I consider Fitted Forecast to be a better term and in my view more intuitively understandable. The Fitted Forecast, when compared to history, over time, shows visually how well the forecast used has been predicting history, or could have predicted history.

3. *Calculated Forecast*: The green line you will see in the user interface screen shots. For those with the black and white version of this book, this line is always ahead of the "current" date. The Calculated Forecast is produced by the application based on the data that is in the Resultant History. The forecast is always based upon Resultant History, because we want the forecast to work off of history plus adjustments, and not just the history.

4. *Synchronized Forecast*: The blue line you will see in the user interface screen shots is the Synchronized Forecast. It is the result of a hierarchy of forecasts and adjustment measures.[3] Because of what I will be showing, the Synchronized Forecast is not the forecast. The Calculated Forecast is a focus, but only for those adjustments to future promotions.

Forecasting Application Fields/Terms

1. *Fitted R-Square:* R-Squared is a measure of the predictive power of a forecasting model. Values range from zero to 1. An R-Squared of 1 means that 100 percent of the variability is explained by the model. It is calculated by comparing the sum of the squared deviations of the forecast with the variance of the series itself. The R-Squared is automatically set to zero if the current calculated forecast would be outperformed by the series mean.

2. *Fitted MAPE:* MAPE stands for Mean Absolute Percent Error. It is a statistical measure of fitted forecast accuracy. This is probably the most common forecast error calculation, and I think the most intuitive. As the name implies, it is equal to the average of the absolute percent errors for all periods. The fitted portion indicates that the calculation is the MAPE of the fitted forecast, which is averaged for the entire time series. (As a note, the fitted MAPE is not reliable for a grouping of products. The fitted MAPE is useful when a single PLC is selected.)

---

[3] The paper copy of this book is printed in black and white; while the colors will not be apparent, their meaning will be easy to discern, especially as there is legend in each screen shot of Smoothie. In the electronic copy of this book, the colors are visible.

3. *Fitted RMSE:* This stands for Root Mean Squared Error and measures variability of the actual sales history versus the forecast. Primarily we will be using this to compare against the Fitted RMSE No Outliers, to show how the forecast accuracy improves when outliers (typically spikes in demand) are removed.

4. *Fitted RMSE No Outliers:* The RMSE with outliers removed. This time-saving statistic does the job of estimating what the forecast error could be without outliers, and automatically identifies all outliers based upon the settings entered into the forecasting application by the user. Therefore, an outlier's distance from the average is controlled by the model setup.

5. *Series Standard Deviation:* Series standard deviation is the standard deviation of all observations (obtained from resultant history and ignoring leading periods with zero demand). Standard deviation is a commonly used measure of variability that measures the variability of forecast relative to the mean.

6. *Series Mean:* Series Mean is the average of all observations (obtained from resultant history and ignoring leading periods with zero demand).

Definitions in this section were partially taken from the Demand Works *Smoothie Help Manual.*

In the black and white versions of the book, I call out and describe what each line represents. As such, it is obvious which line is which. In addition to graphical elements, there are several terms that I will use and that are calculated by the application, and understanding them is important to understanding the analysis. So let's go over them now.

The SCM Focus Site

As I am also the managing editor of the SCM Focus site, http://www.scmfocus.com, the site and the book share a number of concepts and graphics. Furthermore, this book contains many links to articles on the site, which provide more detail on specific subjects. This book provides an explanation of how supply and production planning software works and aims to continue to be a reference after its initial reading. However, if your interest in supply planning software continues to grow, the SCM Focus site is a good resource to which articles are continually added.

The SCM site dedicated specifically to demand planning is http://www.scmfocus.com/demandplanning

Intended Audience

This book is appropriate for anyone who wants to know how to leverage the combination of statistical and sales forecasting. Material in this book will appeal to executives as well as the people who do the work of forecasting. The book is of interest to people in Supply Chain as well as Sales/Marketing, as it addresses both types of forecasting. In fact, this book can help individuals within these groups understand the overall process, as well as how the other side works. If you have any questions or comments on the book, please e-mail me at shaunsnapp@scmfocus.com.

Abbreviations

A listing of all abbreviations used throughout the book is provided at the end of the book.

Corrections

Corrections and updates, as well as reader comments, can be viewed in the comment section of this book's web page. If you have comments or questions, please add them to the following link:

http://www.scmfocus.com/scmfocuspress/forecasting/sales-and-statistical-forecasting-combined/

CHAPTER 2

Where Forecasting Fits within the Supply Chain Planning Footprint

Background

Demand planning is the starting point and first process to be performed in supply chain planning as everything starts with what is the expected demand. The reason for forecasting is simply that the lead times for production and procurement are longer than the customer demand lead-time. Not all companies need to forecast the demand of their products. For example, defense contractors frequently know years in advance what they will be building because they have firm government contracts that contain quantities and dates. However, even these companies are still required to create forecasts for the service parts that support the products they sell.

There is a great deal of discussion about build-to-order (where no forecast is required); the concept is extremely appealing to many companies as it certainly reduces the complexity of the supply chain planning process. Some environments that traditionally "built to stock" are moving towards "build-to-order." An example is book publishing, where books can now be printed in batches of one—at a higher price and a lower quality of course. However, it is not possible for the vast majority of companies to move to a build-to-order environment. Except for extremely specialized manufacturing (such as print-on-demand publishing), it's difficult to come up with examples of products that cost the same amount to produce whether making one or a hundred or a thousand. Similar limitations apply to procurement, as procuring in larger batches is less expensive than procuring in smaller batches. Unless a customer is willing to provide their order in advance, the creation of a physical thing requires a lead-time. As such, there are in fact very few build-to-order environments. Most environments that people call "build-to-order" are actually "assemble-to-order." However, assemble to order still requires a forecast at the subcomponent level. This is why companies must forecast.

Demand Planning Software within Supply Chain Software

The different types of software that comprise demand planning will be described in this book. But first it is important to understand where demand planning fits among the different supply chain applications, as shown in the graphic below.

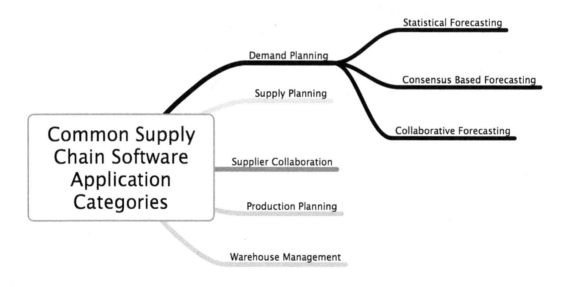

Demand planning one of the major categories of supply chain software. When companies implement an external supply chain planning module to be connected to their ERP system, they most often start with demand planning.

Within the demand planning software category there are three major subcategories. While many supply chain professionals don't know it, each forecasting subcategory has its own specialized software, and this is critical to understand. Companies frequently choose a forecasting application that they think is designed for one category of demand planning, when in fact it was designed for another category. This problem is described in Chapter 13: "Why Companies Select the Wrong Forecasting Software."

The Demand Planning Application Categories

As with other categories of supply chain planning software, over time the demand planning categories have become more defined and more specialized vendors have matured to address different processes. These demand planning categories are listed in the graphic below.

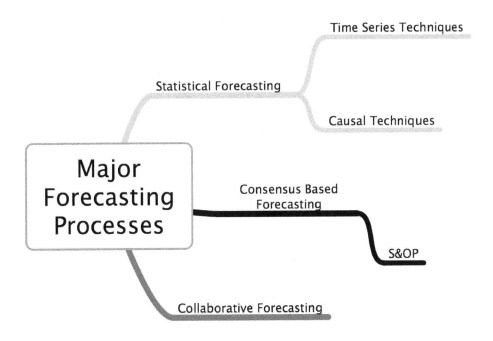

I anticipate that this graphic will be controversial with respect to the location of sales and operations planning (S&OP). Some people think that consensus-based forecasting (CBF) is a subcategory of S&OP. While there is no perfect answer to this question, placing CBF as a subcategory of S&OP is not the most accurate way to depict the relationship between S&OP and CBF.

CBF is used for more than just S&OP. Consensus forecasting systems gather input from multiple human sources within one company in order to drive to a forecast based upon a consensus. S&OP is a high-level forecasting process that deals in dollars and is a consensus forecasting method that involves individuals in sales, operations and finance. However, S&OP is only one type of consensus forecasting performed in a company; companies use consensus processes to develop forecasts at all different levels of the product hierarchy, which have nothing to do with the S&OP forecast.

For these reasons, I have S&OP listed as a subcategory of CBF. However, the categorization discussion does not end there, because S&OP is not only a forecasting process, but is also a capacity planning process, as well as a constraint evaluation process. The S&OP process is (or is supposed to be) the most integrative of planning processes, so it cuts across the supply chain domains of demand planning, supply planning and production planning.

Collaborative forecasting is the final type of forecasting covered in this book. Collaborative forecasting is quite similar to consensus-based forecasting in several respects but involves obtaining inputs from outside of the company. The concept behind collaborative forecasting is that customers and suppliers can help drive improved forecast accuracy by providing their input and data to the company in question.

The Forecast Category, Method and Model Employed

Below the demand planning category, as shown in the previous graphic, is the method (sometimes-called methodology) that is used. Statistical forecasting is a demand planning category; however it employs methods, such as time series methods. Exponential smoothing is one of the times series methods. When the exact parameters are assigned, this becomes a forecasting model. Therefore, the hierarchy is as follows:

- Forecast Category
- Forecast Method
- Forecast Model

However, this hierarchy does not apply the same way to consensus-based forecasting or to collaborative forecasting. For instance, the Delphi Technique is one CBF method. But, we don't typically discuss CBF "models." Collaborative forecasting does not include many methods. CPFR (Collaborative Planning Forecasting and Replenishment) is the best-known method within the collaborative forecasting category. I am not aware of any collaborative forecasting models, because collaborative forecasting is about sharing forecasts that have already been created using some type of statistical model or judgment technique or both.

Simple Arithmetic (last period + two periods ago, etc..) Methods

Time Series Forecasting Category

Exponential Smoothing (earlier, middle or later periods given different weights) Methods

The graphic above shows the methods that are part of the statistical forecasting category.

Some applications can calculate and show what percentage of the product database uses each method. These methods can be assigned to the product or product location using best-fit functionality. Best-fit functionality is a software procedure that runs different forecasting models using past history and compares their forecast results to actuals. It then ranks the different models based upon their distance from the actuals, or their forecast error. The forecasting model with the lowest overall error (a combination of all the individual errors for every period) is then selected, and that is the "best fit." Best-fit functionality can be automated within the application (and run as soon as the application is loaded with data), or can be run as a procedure. Best-fit procedures can only say what the best forecast model would have been in the past, and cannot be said definitively to be the best model to use in the future. Quite often, more complex methods can be made to better fit the history than simpler methods. We will see best-fit forecasting again in Chapter 3: "Statistical Forecasting Explained."

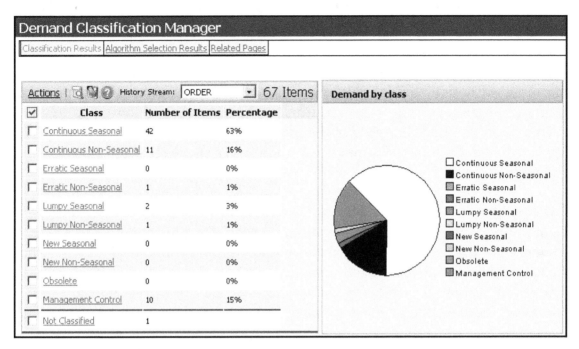

In JDA's DM Classification Manager, it is clear that with this data, the majority of the product database goes out on the continuous non-seasonal method. What is shown in the graphic above are not models, because within each method are multiple models which contain specific configuration details. For instance; a moving average is a method; however a three-period moving average is a specific model.

Connecting the Demand Planning System to Supply Planning

The focus of this book is predominately on demand planning applications, which are separate from ERP systems. ERP systems offer basic demand planning, and while most companies find the ERP demand planning inadequate for their needs, some use only ERP-based demand planning. Because of this fact, there are two system connections between the demand planning system and the supply planning system.

1. The ERP demand planning module connects to the (usually MRP/DRP) supply planning module within the ERP system.

2. The demand planning APS forecast is sent to the supply planning APS. The forecast finds its way to the ERP system indirectly through the re-

lease of the supply plan to the ERP system (although there are several different options here as well).[1]

It is now quite common to have an external APS for both demand and supply planning, although this is more common for larger than smaller companies. Demand planning tends to be the first application that is moved to an APS system, and demand planning is the most commonly purchased and installed application/module in the supply chain planning space. It also tends to have the highest executive profile.

Conclusion

Demand planning is one of the major categories of supply chain software. It is composed of three different categories of demand planning, each of which has specifically designed software. Statistical forecasting was the first forecasting process to be placed into software and sold to the enterprise market, and it serves as the baseline or main point of reference for many supply chain professionals as to what forecasting software should "look like." However, using the design of statistical forecasting applications to generalize towards other categories of demand planning software is not good practice. Therefore, the most common misapplication of a category of demand planning software is typically when a statistical forecasting application is used for consensus or collaborative forecasting. This bears emphasis: there is not simply "one type" of demand planning process in supply chain management. Each forecasting process may not absolutely require a customize application, but in practice is often optimized by a different software design, and there is no single forecasting application that handles all of the forecasting processes equally well. This book will describe all the processes and explain the different forecasting application categories.

---

[1] Another possibility is to connect the non-ERP demand planning system (often referred to as advanced planning and scheduling [APS]) to the ERP supply planning module. However, this is very rarely done.

CHAPTER 3

The Common Problems with Statistical Forecasting

Statistical forecasting is the use of a mathematical method to attempt to reproduce a pattern from the demand history. The majority of enterprise software that is purchased and implemented for forecasting is for statistical forecasting.

The following are some interesting features of statistical forecasting.

1. *General Availability of Information:* Books on statistical forecasting have been available for many years.

2. *Academic Education:* Statistical forecasting is taught at universities, although the university one attends determines the availability of courses. Most people can benefit from a forecasting class after they have already graduated from college.

3. *Availability of Applications:* Many companies have purchased specialized statistical forecasting applications, making them generally available. However, the features of statistical forecasting applications vary significantly from vendor to vendor. The popularity of any statistical forecasting application does

not appear to be correlated with its functionality (at least, not as I rate functionality). Those companies that attempt to perform statistical forecasting from their ERP systems tend to have poor statistical forecasting outcomes.

4. *Encapsulated Forecasting Methods:* Many advanced forecasting methods are available within applications, allowing for a level of complexity that in all likelihood could not be used effectively without the applications.

5. *Familiarity with Forecasting Terminology:* Many people are familiar with forecasting terminology, such as exponential smoothing, forecasting parameters, etc. Still, technical forecasting knowledge beyond what I would consider basic knowledge is not common, even within forecasting departments.

On the surface, the dissemination of information about statistical forecasting seems to have been accomplished. I have consulted and worked in many forecasting environments, and in my opinion the ability of companies to leverage their investment into statistical forecasting continues to be poor, even with the availability of information, and it does not seem to show many signs of improving.[1] Within these companies, it is exceedingly rare to find people who not only know the individual ingredients of forecasting, but who understand how to assemble the ingredients into a "meal." Thus, there is a wide chasm between the capabilities of applications that are described on software vendor websites and what is actually implemented in companies. While this statement generalizes to many other software categories, I am focusing on statistical forecasting here and want to address the issues specific to statistical forecasting that prevent it from achieving its potential.

---

[1] This fact seems to be greatly underemphasized in the literature. Essentially there is little incentive to bring this fact to the surface. Software vendors don't want this known, because it may dampen demand. Academics, unless they perform significant consulting work, don't know the forecasting level in industry, and consultants tend to want to promote rather than "bring people down with the reality of the situation."

Applying the Historical Approach to Systems Implementation

My philosophy to systems implementation might seem logical, but is actually quite unfashionable:

Strategies, tactics, and approaches should be adjusted in light of **what occurred before**.

Let's call my philosophy the historical approach to software implementation. Because it depends on a feedback loop between previous implementations and adjustments to the approach used (and this feedback loop tends to be poor in most companies), this approach is not followed widely.

IT implementations have a high failure rate. People offer a variety of opinions as to why this is so, but one reason I don't hear is that the approaches to both software selection and software implementation **change little from year to year**. This topic is truly caught in a time warp. I simply cannot believe that so little modification has been made to how software is implemented, particularly in light of the well-known failures caused by using the flawed approaches. And hiring a specialist in implementation often does not seem to help, because many of these companies also refuse to learn, adapt, and adjust. I have been quite disappointed in the lack of learning on the part of consulting companies from previous implementations. The more common strategy is to repeat the mistakes from the past, while simultaneously changing the buzzwords. I have seen the following common mistakes made during statistical forecasting projects:

1. *Maintenance Mismatch*: The company purchases an application, and the maintenance it requires is higher than the company's ability to commit resources to supporting it.

2. *Purchasing the Wrong Forecasting Application*: In my experience, it is often the case that a company will have selected an application that is a poor fit for its needs, as explained in the following article: http://www.scmfocus.com/demandplanning/2010/09/why-companies-are-selecting-the-wrong-supply-chain-demand-planning-systems/.[2]

---

[2] I cover this in more detail in the SCM Focus Press book *Supply Chain Forecasting Software*.

3. *Too Few Automated Procedures Used*: Companies often have thousands or hundreds of thousands of PLCs. It is not possible to manually forecast a very large number of PLCs, and it is important to leverage automated procedures—such as best fit—which will be covered in Chapter 4: "Best Fit Forecasting." Much of the heavy lifting in forecasting should be performed by automated procedures of this nature. This issue generalizes outside of forecasting to other types of supply chain planning, such as how master data inventory parameters are set in the supply and production planning area.[3]

4. *Lack of True Attribute-based Forecasting Systems*: Many forecasting systems have weak attribute functionality, even though attributes are critical to controlling a database of PLCs. Attribute functionality differs greatly by application, and while many applications "have" attribute-based functionality, few excel at its use. Attributes functionality for forecasting is identical to attribute functionality in business intelligence. However, not enough software vendors have made business intelligence controllable by the business users for building the attribute relationships. Therefore, business intelligence and forecasting applications tend to require many man-hours to obtain the required output. This is a matter of software design, because there are some applications where attributes can be adjusted relatively easily. Unfortunately, companies generally cannot differentiate between weak attribute functionality and strong attribute functionality, and most do not appreciate the importance of attributes in determining what the forecasting system will eventually be able to do.

5. *Under Staffing*: Under staffing the position of forecasting with low cost resources (but not sufficiently educated or experienced resources) is associated with not adjusting the staffing to the requirements of the application. Companies do not value the forecasting role in a way that is commensurate with the ability of forecasting to **add value** to the company.

---

[3] Many inventory parameters, such as lot size and safety stock, tend to be set in very antiquated ways, and are often changed independently in order to solve a short-term problem. The sub site at SCM Focus, http://www.scmfocus.com/3S/ explains how these values should actually be set to get the most from these systems.

Companies rarely appreciate the full costs of low forecast accuracy.[4] If they could quantify the amount of money they are losing by sub-optimizing their forecasting, they would be more willing to part with money to solve the problem. I have performed this type of quantification for companies, but it is always an uphill battle to get the appropriate investment into forecasting. It seems that companies require extraordinary evidence to properly fund forecasting departments; meanwhile, new resources can be hired in Sales or Marketing with far less evidence because they "increase sales."

6. *Lack of Testing*: System testing, such as making sure the environment is stable before migrating between computer hardware, can be an issue, but that is not the type of testing I am describing in this case. Instead, I am describing the lack of testing of the effectiveness of various approaches for particular PLCs. Far too many companies, enabled by software salespeople, see the forecasting system as something that is so magical that they don't have to apply very much effort to get it to work properly. It's not one or the other. No forecasting application, no matter how fancy (current buzzwords include "machine learning" and "fuzzy algorithms") is going to operate properly without a significant investment from people. Software vendors that pitch their applications as "deskilling the forecasting position" or allowing the company to cut demand planning resources as a carrot to enable the company to "fund the software acqui-

---

[4] Improved forecast accuracy is extremely valuable to companies. However, companies tend keep the purse strings closed when it comes to resources unless they are managing a group of forecasters. This is a major error. A talented demand planning resource— one who knows his or her trade and can extract the most from the forecasting systems and can work to get various inputs into the system from other sources—is extremely valuable. Better forecasting means many positive outcomes that typically lead to sales growth, including being in-stock more often, higher services levels, less rework, and being considered as a more reliable supplier. Salespeople constantly state that if they only had a better service level, they could make more sales. That service level improvement begins at forecasting. To become good at forecasting, one has to have experience and augment his or her knowledge with the conceptual foundations of forecasting. To become very good at it requires work, and the incentive must be in place to do it. Too many companies see forecasting as a junior function, where the main way to improve one's income is to be promoted into the managing forecasting group. Companies that take the technical knowledge of forecasting for granted, or devalue it in relation to other roles or to the management of forecasting will pay the price with higher forecast errors.

sition," should really be ashamed of themselves. The forecasting function is staffed at such a low level at the vast majority of companies that the only correct answer is to increase, not decrease, the staffing level.

7. *Data Maintenance*: Not properly maintaining forecast history is a fairly common occurrence, and this breaks into many subcategories:

   a. *Missing Periods:* Having many periods of zero demand in the sales history. When companies stock-out they will show zero demand for that month. However, was that **really** a period of no demand? This is why a forecast method should not be based off of the actual history, but instead upon the adjusted history, or what will be referred to in this book as the Resultant History.

   b. *Historical Substitution:* Not performing historical substitution of the sales history of discontinued items to their new counterparts.

   c. *Promotions:* Not accounting for promotions in the sales history (a topic covered in my book *Promotions Forecasting: Techniques of Forecast Adjustments in Software*).

   d. *Multiple Forecasts and Multiple Demand Histories:* If a company does not store its multiple forecasts, it cannot perform a comparison among the various approaches used and cannot develop a strategy for various PLCs.

Data Quality

The way statistical forecasting works is that the forecasting system applies a forecasting method to the demand history or time series. Statistical forecasting is so-named because it does not simply reproduce what happened in the past, but instead uses statistics to determine what part of the past periods (the population) to sample (that is, to take and reproduce for the future). Let's explain this with some concrete examples:

Product A: Demand History

Jan	Feb	Mar	Apr	May	June	July	Aug	Sep	Oct	Nov	Dec
20	23	13	5	3	33	25	28	45	41	23	21

Graphically, the demand history looks like the following:

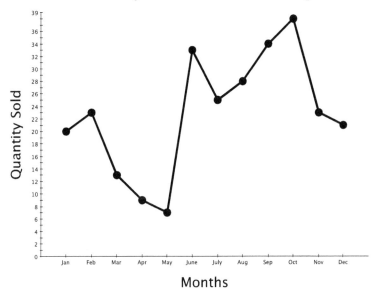

Now what happens if, because of data quality issues, three periods of demand (April, May and October) are simply missing from the history?

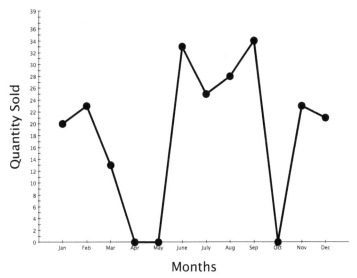

This demand history looks entirely different. The forecasting system will interpret any blank values as zeros (unless adjusted for or unless the system has the functionality to ignore zero values), and will attempt to replicate this "history" into the forecast.

Now let's take a look at another example of a data problem. Because companies often introduce many new products (many of which are just slight variations of old products), and because many companies do not associate the old history with the new product number, the forecasting system will very frequently see a demand history that looks like this.

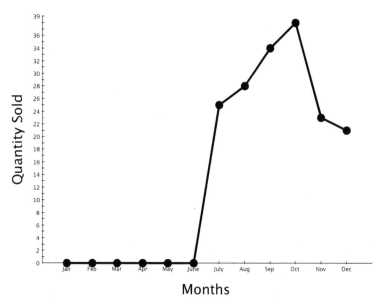

Months

*Unless this is a new product, clearly this is not the actual history. But the statistical forecasting system **does not know this;** it assumes you are telling it the truth— there was no demand from Jan to June. After several periods have passed (say, up until September), the system will see this is a very fast growing item and will attempt to project the forecast very high for October, November and December, and of course that would be the wrong decision to make.*

One of the problems is that **so much** of the data history that some companies use to perform forecasting is **not useful** for statistical forecasting, which brings up the topic of forecast-ability. Forecast-ability is essentially the measurement of how well a forecast method can predict the future. One important measure of forecast-ability is called the Fitted R-Square. This is the predictive power of a forecasting model.

Production Versus Research or Laboratory Environments

When it comes to the evaluation of forecasting software, it is important to understand the distinction between a laboratory environment and production environment. A laboratory environment is where new ideas are tested. A production environment is where older, tested approaches are put to use.

In a pure "laboratory environment," a particular approach system could produce a superior result.[5] However, no company I have ever consulted for has ever had a laboratory environment; in fact, they are just the opposite—they are production environments that require easy-to-use applications with low maintenance requirements and a low incidence of breakdown. Also, while those who perform forecasting research tend to have PhDs in mathematics, those who work in forecasting for companies do not (and quite often have little in the way of training in forecasting either). In the real world, most training takes place on the job and the best that can normally be expected is that the resource will complete APICS training on his or her own time.

---

[5] Actually, this is a problem with many forecasting studies. In the study, a complex forecasting method is tested and it is determined that it can outperform a simpler forecasting method. However, what is left out of the analysis is how much work it takes to implement and tune the more complex forecasting method. Most forecast studies only use a few products; that is, they apply a laboratory environment to the problem. However, when implemented in production environments, thousands of items must be forecasted, and each product cannot receive the type of attention that can be given to an item in a laboratory or research environment. This is one reason why new and advanced forecasting methods do not match the forecast accuracy benefits that academic research papers predict.

Back in the 1970s and 1980s, there was great optimism that the computerization of complex forecast methods would easily lead to high quality forecasts. This was the height of optimism regarding the potential of black-box forecasting systems. The thought was that data would simply go in and the mathematics would do all the heavy lifting. A contingent of those in academics, and others with deep forecasting expertise, believed that forecasting issues had been solved; for the first time, computers could apply methods that could never have been applied with manual calculation.

The outcome was that very complex methods did not improve forecasting much. As it turned out, there was much more to better forecasting than the application of complex algorithms; rather embarrassingly, many of the simple methods beat the complex methods in actual practice. Many software vendors do not seem to have learned from this history, and continue to present forecasting as simply a matter of the application of mathematical models.

One cannot certify an application or approach in a laboratory environment and based solely on that, **declare it** to be appropriate for a production environment. Research is performed in a laboratory environment because this is where creative work is performed, software is developed, and controls can be put into place. After the desirable features are selected and tuned, the step before putting the application into production is generally referred to as "field-testing." It is important to avoid creating complex solutions in a laboratory environment that do not translate to a production environment. One must match the approach for where the approach will be used, not where the approach was developed. I explain the results of a poorly field-tested supply chain application in the following quotation from *Supply Chain Forecasting Software*:

> *"In many cases, enterprise-forecasting software is not anywhere as easy to use as it could be. Users tend to naturally gravitate away from using software that does not serve them. I was once in a meeting where the project decision makers, frustrated that the users were using Excel rather than the expensive planning system they had implemented, briefly discussed the feasibility of removing Excel from the planners' computers as a way to force them to use the expensive forecasting system."*

It should be remembered that the value of a statistical forecasting application is only partially in its models (exponential smoothing, seasonal, level, etc.). Other areas such as data management and the ability to perform forecast adjustments are just as important. These are the capabilities that many companies are truly missing and that prevent many companies from leveraging the forecast methods within their forecasting applications.

In summary, the ability to perform, record and report on forecast adjustments should be improved. This is true even if the statistical forecast is improved and fewer forecast adjustments are required.

The Real State of Statistical Forecasting

The sad fact is that many statistical forecasting processes and systems across the US and internationally are in a state of disrepair. The software salespeople sold the dream, the consultants made their money, but the statistical forecasting system is not a big part of the forecasting process. This is always evident, because in these environments, the sales forecast becomes predominant, and Sales/Marketing is constantly being prompted to provide their forecasts. Because so many companies cannot master statistical forecasting, they over-rely on Sales to provide the forecast. The argument is often made that, *"Sales should do the forecasting as they are closest to the customer."* However, research in this area—as well as my consulting experience dealing with many forecasting data sets—indicate that Sales does not always add value to the forecast. Sales and Marketing may add value to some of the PLCs (but not necessarily all of the PLCs); the company should know definitively which of the PLCs falls into which category. This is why it's better to rely upon testing than guesswork when it comes to managing the PLC database for forecasting purposes. The topic of testing is covered further on in this book.

Conclusion

Statistical forecasting is the use of a mathematical method to attempt to reproduce a pattern from the demand history. Consulting companies and implementing companies in general do a very poor job of using the history of demand planning implementations to change their approach. In this chapter I laid out some of the common issues with demand planning implementation with a focus on getting readers to focus specifically on addressing these issues in future implementations. A very important distinction for demand planning implementations is between laboratory environments versus production environments, New forecasting approaches and mathematics tend to be created in laboratory environments, but being able to show improvement in a laboratory environment does not prove that the innovation can be applied equally effectively in a production environment. In fact, in most cases the innovation will be less effective in a production environment.

CHAPTER 4

Introduction to Best Fit Forecasting

Recently I performed keyword research for common forecasting terms, and it was quite surprising to find the very low number of searches for the term "best fit forecasting." Best fit forecasting is a very important technique for simplifying statistical forecasting and for improving the ability of companies to leverage statistical forecasting. It has been around for quite some time, but is often still not fully leveraged in industry.

Best fit is a software procedure that fits the past history using different forecasting models. It then ranks the different models based upon their distance from the actuals, or their forecast error. The forecast model with the lowest overall error is then selected (the overall error is a combination of all the individual errors for every period), and that is the "best fit." Best fit functionality can be automated within the application (that is, run as soon as the application is loaded with data), or best fit can run interactively or as a background job, and how best fit is run varies depending upon the particular application. Best fit procedures can only say what the **best forecast model would have been in the past, and not what the best model would be to use in the future**. Often, more complex methods can be made to better fit the history than simpler methods.

The best fit procedure is so important because companies that engage in supply chain management typically have thousands to hundreds of thousands of individual product-location combinations, and in most cases each one of these product-location combinations requires a forecast. This is a lot of line items to keep up with, and a big part of forecast accuracy is choosing the right forecasting model. Best fit allows the selection of the right forecasting model to be performed in an automated fashion (depending upon the models available within the application, which we will discuss in detail in this chapter). Just as importantly, best fit can change the model selected each time the forecast is calculated, which means that as the products change (as new products are substituted for old products, and so on), the forecasting model can change. When done properly, best fit forecasting holds the keys for improving many—but certainly not all—of the problems associated with statistical forecasting.

Overestimating Best Fit Forecasting

Many people think that best fit forecasting is simply a functionality that can be activated within a forecasting application, and that's all there is to it. Companies have a predisposition to believe this; they would like to have the most sophisticated functionality possible, functionality that adds the most possible value to their business, and that basically **runs itself**. I work in advanced planning; I have worked with the most sophisticated technology in supply chain planning, and this belief—that complex systems can be implemented by people with average skill and maintained with below average resource commitment (a position that is proposed by the salespeople at software vendors in order to maximize their sales)—is in my view a primary reason why so few companies have been able to get the promised value out of the systems they purchased.

In the systems I analyze, it is quite easy to find areas where the system has either not been configured correctly, or where the system is otherwise sub-optimized. It's not a question **if** I will find a major area of the software that is not properly implemented or maintained, but **which area it will be**. Best fit forecasting, for reasons I will explain in detail, does not simply work automatically. It requires skill and thorough testing in order to manage the functionality in a best-fit forecasting application. This book will provide the story that you will not hear from software vendors or from many consultants.

Common Problems with Best Fit Forecasting Functionality

A common problem with best-fit functionality is that most companies end up with forecasting software that has too much overhead to run best fit. In addition, best-fit functionality must be controlled to prevent what is known as **over-fitting**. The best-fit procedure that a forecasting application uses (and different applications have different mathematics that control the procedure's outcome) can only tell the user what forecasting models would have worked in the past. Sometimes this is the forecasting model that should be used in the future, but in many cases it should not be used. Fitting history is easy; the difficult part is forecasting accurately, as is emphasized by the well-regarded author, Michael Gilliland of SAS.

> *"Historical fit is virtually always better than the accuracy of the forecasts generated. In many situations the historical fit is better than the accuracy of the forecasts. Any one of you who has done statistical forecasting knows this. You might have a MAPE of 5 percent in your historical fit, but a MAPE of 50 percent in your forecasts—that would not be at all unusual. As a practical and career-extending suggestion in communicating with your management, don't tell them the MAPE of your historical fit— they don't need to know it! Knowing the MAPE of your historical fit will only lead to unrealistic expectations about the accuracy of your future forecasts."*

Now we will look an example of this exact issue within a forecasting application.

Best Fit and Over fitting

The screen shot below shows a PLC for which a best-fit procedure has been run and a forecasting model automatically assigned.

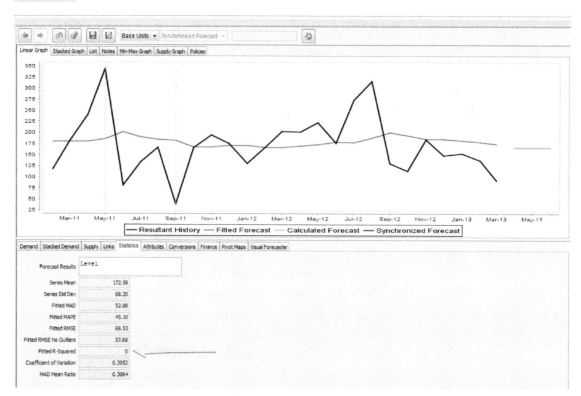

The forecasting system has also assigned a Fitted R-Square of zero. This is how we know (although we can also tell by the graph) that the best fit procedure that was run on this item was not able to find a pattern that it thinks can be relied upon to produce a forecast. Therefore it chooses a Level forecast model. Zero is the lowest value any data set can attain in terms of forecast-ability. However, we have a very large outlier, which is degrading our forecast statistics.

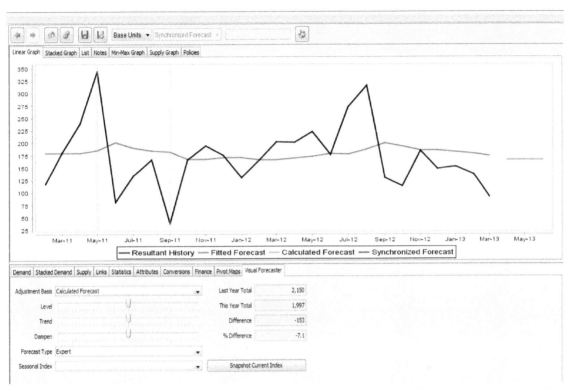

The screen shot above is a best fit forecast created in a modern forecasting system. The Forecast Type is set to "Expert," which in this particular application means that the application is selecting what it thinks is the best forecasting model to apply to the PLC (each application uses slightly different terminology). However, notice that there is not a very good match between the Resultant History (the black line) and the red line, which is the Fitted Forecast produced by the forecasting system. In this case I would switch the model to a seasonal pattern, which is a better method for this product's demand history. I do this by changing the Forecast Type to "Seasonal." Notice in the next screen shot how much closer the red line and the black line are to one another.

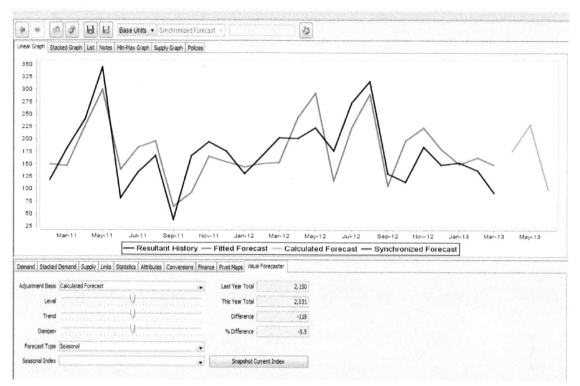

The Fitted Forecast is now much closer to the Resultant History. And if we check the statistics, the Fitted R-Square is much higher.

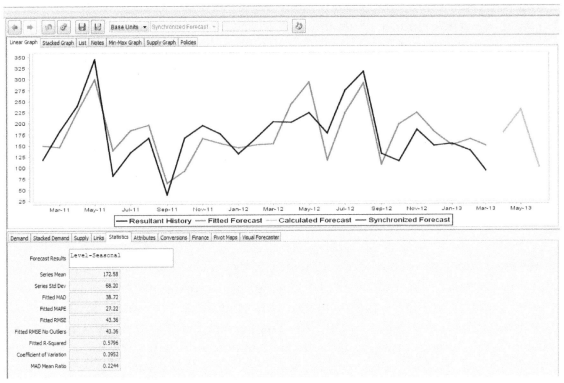

However, is this the right forecasting model or are we engaging in over-fitting?

In my book *Supply Chain Forecasting Software,* I make the point that a portion of the product database should be identified as unforecastable, and when this is the case, the forecast method that is used is a level or constant forecast. In his book, Michael Gilliland of SAS makes a similar point when he describes "over-fitting," which means either developing a custom forecasting model, or using best fit functionality in an application in a unifocal manner only, in an attempt to fit the model to the demand history:

> *"But fit to history should not be the sole consideration when choosing your forecasting model. Blindly choosing the best fitting model and assuming it is the most appropriate for forecasting can be a problem in some forecasting packages, or in the misuse of those packages. Remember again that our objective is to create good forecasts...The key point for selection should not be the fit of the model, but the appropriateness of the model to the nature of behavior you are trying to forecast."*

He then uses the example of attempting to predict the results of flipping a coin, which of course cannot be predicted.

> *"You could fit a sophisticated model to this pattern. You could even fit the pattern perfectly and project it into the next year. But this is not the right forecast. You would have over fit such a model to the randomness. The proper model in this case is a straight line at 50 percent heads. Even though its fit to the history is not great and it won't forecast particularly well, 50 percent heads is still the most appropriate forecast to use. It will deliver the most accurate and unbiased forecast possible over time."*

What is so effective is that Michael uses the example of something that is ridiculous to forecast: the forecasting of the unforecastable—coin flips. Obviously, a level forecast is the best forecast in this situation, because a level forecast would always choose a head or a tail. The reason for this is that it is not possible to beat the odds by trying to predict which side will turn up next. If the coin is honest, the sequence of heads and tails will tend to match a random sequence, which if enough flips are made, will tend to approximate 50 percent heads and 50 percent tails. However, Michael states that a very complex model can be used to perfectly model a random activity and can also be used to perfectly model or fit the history of anything. For items that are difficult to forecast, the whole point is that **a replica of the past will not forecast the future.**

While Michael's example is purposefully ridiculous, this is no joke. People attempt to forecast unforecastable things all the time, and to use a lot of math (or smoke and mirrors) to cover up the fact that the item of interest is not forecastable. This is one of the reasons why Wall Street employs so many mathematicians. Complicated math is in essence the new mysticism. In order for anything to be considered mystic, is must be incomprehensible but have an aura of legitimacy. This belief extends to kings who once consulted mystics or oracles as to the results of battles, weather, or the harvest, and in the present day it extends to math— as long as it's sufficiently complicated so that not many people understand it.

With all of this in mind, let's go back to the example of the increased Fitted R-Square of applying a seasonal model.

The question is, should we model or fit as closely as possible to history, or take more of an average approach, which is proposed by the best fit procedure of the forecasting application.

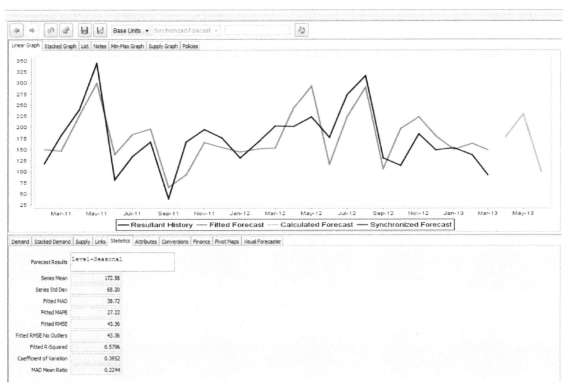

Notice that the fit between the Resultant History (black line) and Fitted Forecast (what the system would have forecasted for every period) is not very high. A seasonal method will fit much better. However, should a seasonal pattern be used? That depends upon whether the right answer is to weigh previous history or more recent history more heavily. This is where domain expertise can be leveraged.

*All that a statistical forecasting method knows is what it's told. For instance if Sales/ Marketing knows that there was a reason that the expected peak in May did not occur, and that the seasonal pattern is set to re-emerge, then the best fit method can be **overridden permanently** with a seasonal pattern. However, perhaps there is a different explanation. What if all of the seasonality was controlled by promotions and in May* *there was no promotion. If promotions were accounted for along with the demand history, then the forecasting system would have the* **necessary information** *to create a better forecast, and the forecasting application would switch forecasting models very quickly. I cover how to account for promotions in the demand history and how to forecast promotions in the book Promotions Forecasting: Techniques of Forecast Adjustments in Software.*

I hope these screen shots have demonstrated that running best fit functionality should not be a time-consuming or high-maintenance activity, which is the experience that many companies have with their forecasting applications.[1]

Furthermore, while companies only address the question of when to enable the best fit functionality and when to enable another manually determined forecasting approach, there are in fact other questions they should be asking. I have seen companies struggle with running a best-fit procedure when they have persistent data problems in their demand history. Data inaccuracies need to be addressed before best-fit procedure is run. I have seen companies come to the conclusion that the reason best fit procedure in their application was not working properly was due to poor sales history quality.

Conclusion

Considering its importance, best fit forecasting is far less well known than it should be. Best fit is a software procedure that fits the past history using different forecasting models. It then ranks the different models based upon their distance from the actuals, or their "forecast error." The forecast model with the lowest overall error is then selected (the overall error is a combination of all the individual errors for every period), and that is the "best fit." The best fit procedure is so important because companies that engage in supply chain management typically have thousands to hundreds of thousands of individual product-location combinations, and in most cases each one of these product-location combinations requires a forecast. This is a lot of line items to keep up with, and a big part of forecast accuracy is choosing the right forecasting mod-

---

[1] Let's also remember that during the software sales process, most likely the ability to run multiple forecasting models was emphasized as being something easy and straightforward to do.

el. Software vendors tend to explain best fit functionality as functionality that runs itself. This is untrue, and companies that do not provide trained demand planners for their best fit applications generally have problems getting value from best fit forecasting applications. The objective of best fit forecasting is to create the best forecast, but not overfit the sales history. The example of fitting a coin flip was provided to show an extreme example and how a perfectly fitting forecast is not necessarily the forecast your want to use.

CHAPTER 5

Comparing Best Fit Forecasting to Homegrown Statistical Forecasting Models

Another reason why best fit cannot be run without intervention is that a forecasting system does not store in its database every forecasting method in the universe. And it is common for companies to create "home grown" forecasting models that for some PLCs outperform the forecasting model selected by the best-fit system. There is a very specific way of testing best fit forecasting versus statistical models that are not included in the forecasting application.

Managing Best Fit Comparisons

First, a best-fit forecast can be compared against the current forecasting models to see which model has the higher rate of accuracy. While the best fit procedure is very well known in forecasting, upon reflection perhaps best fit should have been called "limited best fit," or "pretty good fit," because the procedure can only find the best fit from among the forecasting models that are **within** its forecasting system database. What is in the database does not constitute the total universe of forecasting models that are actually available to be tested; however, this is often what people think best fit does. Custom forecasting models **are often** developed by companies that are superior in some circumstances to the standard models that are used by forecasting systems. Unfortunately, custom-forecasting models cannot be added to a best fit procedure without coding/customization, and therefore, comparisons between the best fit matching and other forecasting models must be performed outside of the forecasting system. And that is a critical point. This is why best fit cannot simply be run, and then the selected forecast model used in all cases because it may not actually be the best model to use in each case. However, when a new best fit forecast is created for a product database, there must be a way of holding it separate from the other forecasts, and to be able to compare each of these forecasts, and to perform analytics on them in order to understand the differences in forecast accuracy.

Steps in the Best Fit Model to Home Grown Model Comparison Process

As mentioned previously, this book is a cookbook; in this case the overall process of the best-fit comparison will be explained, as well as the detail within each step of the process, in such a way that readers will be able to repeat the process. The following are the steps that I follow in order to compare a best-fit forecasting model to homegrown models.

1. How the PLCs Are Selected

2. The Calculations Used for the High-level Analysis

3. The High-level Analysis

4. The Detailed Analysis

5. Conclusion

How the PLCs Are Selected

Many companies prefer that the PLCs be selected on the basis of the forecast error. The logic for this is that if the PLC has a low forecast error, the current model is probably working for that PLC. Eventually it makes sense to run this comparison for all the PLCs, but it makes a lot of sense to start off with the highest error PLCs, and allows a recommendation to be made more quickly, which can help to provide support for performing this analysis for the overall PLC database. There are two components to this step. One is to determine the forecast error method. This really depends upon what is important to the company.

IF(Forecast Error >.25, 1,0)

In addition to segmenting the PLC database by error level, companies often want to go after the higher volume PLCs with high error first. Of course making changes to the higher volume PLCs will have a stronger effect on the company than lower volume PLCs. So the following formula is a good example.

IF(Forecast Error >.25, IF(12 Months Average of Sales Units >500,1,0)

This threshold filters for product location combinations with a forecast error of more than 25% along with an average of sales greater than 500 units.

This creates a threshold of acceptable forecast accuracy, and identified PLCs that exceeded that boundary. This of course creates a binary value for each PLC for each month. Generally, companies are interested in PLCs that **exceeded the threshold consistently**. Therefore a PLC that exceeds the threshold one time over all of the periods reviewed would not necessarily be analyze, but those that exceeded the threshold more frequently than this would most likely be analyzed. Below is what the matrix would look like for all PLCs for the period that the test is performed.

PLC Selector

Product Category	Product	Avg Monthly Sales	Months Where Error Tolerance is Exceeded for > 500 per Month Average Sales History Items						
			Jan	Feb	Mar	Apr	May	Jun	Total
A	Tuna Fish	500	1	0	1	1	0	0	3
A	Swordfish	600	0	0	0	0	0	0	0
A	Mahi Mahi	320	0	0	1	0	1	0	2

Because the rule is that that any PLC that exceeds the threshold more than twice in the test period, and which also has an average monthly sales history of 500 units, given the assumptions above, only Tunafish would meet both these criteria and be included in the analysis.

The Calculations Used for the High-level Analysis

Here we applied a series of calculations to the sample PLCs. Each calculation is a column in a spreadsheet.

1. *The Percent of the Error Related to Model Selection Total:* In this calculation, the homegrown forecast error of the company was subtracted from the best fit forecast error that I run. I then divided this value by the company's forecast error, which comes from the homegrown forecast model. This provides the percentage of the baseline error that is related to the model selected. (The Excel formula for this is provided below.) From this analysis it can be determined whether the best fit tested forecasting models **or** the company's homegrown forecasting models worked better for each PLC.

2. *Model-related Forecast Error:* This calculation simply returns a 1 if the Percent of Error Related to Model Selection Total was less than 0.

3. *Standard Deviation of the Demand History:* This was a simple standard deviation, which was taken to evaluate the relationship between forecast error and variability. This is a measure of forecast-ability. While not always, time series with higher variability generally have lower forecast-ability than lower variability time series.

4. *Average of the Demand History:* This was used for the variability measurement, as in the next bullet point. It is also used for determining the relationship between forecast error magnitude and the volume of sales for the PLC.

5. *Number of Periods of Demand History with Zero Demand:* This noted how many months of the sales history had zero demand.

Here is the error calculation from step one.

ABS(Homegrown Forecast Error − Best Fit Forecast Error)/Homegrown Forecast Method Forecast Error

The High-level Analysis

Some percentage of the PLCs in the file provided by clients will exceed the threshold. This is the basis for the study sample. We will now review the study sample for a series of statistics, and this will make up the high-level analysis. These statistics will tell us important information regarding how to assign the PLCs to different forecasting methods.

Percent of Error Related to Model Selection Total

Any error that is associated with the model selected was tested by comparing the error percentage of the forecast generated by homegrown models to the forecast **generated by a best-fit procedure**. A company may want this analysis performed for several groups of PLCs. By performing the analysis for a group, one can see the variability or lack of variability in the percentages.

Percentage of PLCs Forecasted Better

	PLC Goup A	PLC Group B	PLC Group C	Average
Frequency with Which Best Fit Procedure Beat Homegrown Model	65%	80%	76%	74%
Frequency with Which Homegrown Beat Model Best Fit Selected Model	35%	20%	24%	26%

*Above is a comparison across three groups of PLCs. It shows how their forecast accuracy compares when they are forecasted with a homegrown forecasting model versus a best fit forecasting model. In PLC Group A, the model selected by best fit forecasting (and this could be any of a number of models that are selected by the best fit procedure) **beats** the homegrown model 65 percent of the time, and this percentage is higher for PLC Group B and PLC Group C.*

Average Forecast Improvement

	PLC Goup A	PLC Group B	PLC Group C	Average
Percent Improvement for Using Best Fit Model When it is Superior	54%	52%	58%	55%
Percent Improvement for Using Homegrown Model When it is Superior	85%	37%	100%	74%

*When a model produces a better forecast, how much more accurate is that forecast than the model selected by the other approach? In the case of PLC Group A, for cases where the best-fit model is superior, there is a **54 percent improvement in forecast accuracy**. However, in the cases where the homegrown model provides a superior forecast, it improves the forecast accuracy by **85 percent versus the best-fit forecasting selected model**.*

This analysis shows that there is a significant opportunity for forecast improvement by **selectively** applying a best-fit procedure forecast method to the PLCs. This generalizes to PLCs that are not in the sample. There are many cases with the lower forecast error PLCs where the best fit procedure will also provide forecast accuracy improvement over some of the homegrown models, but as with the current homegrown method-based forecast, accuracy improves with respect to each PLC.

The conclusion that we can draw here is that the best outcomes will be obtained through a **combination** of the homegrown forecasting methods and the selections made by best-fit assignment. This is accomplished by assigning the forecast models (either the best fit assigned or homegrown methods) to the right PLCs.

Demand history that is more variable is more difficult to predict than demand history that is more stable. Variance is not difficult to forecast if it is perfectly repeating. For instance, a perfectly repeating seasonal pattern may have zero forecast error. However, in most cases variance is **not perfectly repeating,** and this is why variance correlates negatively with forecast-ability. The purpose of comparing the out-of-threshold PLCs to the overall database is to determine how much higher the variance is for the sample versus the average for

PLC database, and therefore how much the variance by itself is to blame for the higher forecast error.

Standard Deviation of the Demand History from

The standard deviation of sales history of the overall database that was used in this example from Dec 2012 to Aug 2013 was **181**. The average of sales history of the overall database that was used from Dec 2012 to Aug 2013 was **483**. This is a ratio of standard deviation to average demand of **.37**. This is the value that I compared against the sample PLCs from each category analyzed.

Variability Comparison

Average Variance of All Sample PLCs			37%	

	PLC Goup A	PLC Group B	PLC Group C	Average
Average Variance of Demand History	39%	61%	132%	77%
Variance Multiple of PLCs Over the Average Variance for the Sample PLCs	1.05	1.65	3.57	2.09

Here we can see that if we average the variance of the categories, compared with the variance of the "mother" data set, these categories have twice the variance.

Number of Periods of Demand History with Zero Demand

Many companies have far too many periods of zero demand in their sales history. This is partially driven by a lack of sales history substitution, where the sales history from an expired PLC is superimposed upon a **new** PLC. But there are other reasons as well, including the fact that some companies frequently will stock out of some PLCs for months, resulting in zero sales for these months. These zero sales are then included into the forecast. (This is an example of where historical adjustment would be useful, and historical adjustment will be repeatedly demonstrated further on in this book. Therefore, when there are a number of zeros in the demand history, unless these were periods where the authentic demand was actually zero (and stocking out does not mean there was no demand, it means there was no supply) then this will reduce forecast accuracy.

Periods of Zero Demand Comparison

	PLC Goup A	PLC Group B	PLC Group C	Average
Periods of Zero Demand	2.0%	1.5%	1.0%	2%

This particular data sample only had a few zeros in each category. Therefore, periods of zero demand were not a driver in the higher forecast inaccuracy.

Conclusion

Homegrown forecasting models are an important set of methods that should be tested against the application's best fit. Homegrown forecasting methods often represent a considerable investment on the part of the companies that have developed them and represent a customized forecast method that is often not available as part of the database of the best fit forecasting functionality.

In this chapter we completed the first step in the process of statistical forecasting; that is we have compared and found the best forecasting method for each SKU through a combination of testing the homegrown forecasting methods against the forecasting models selected by best fit. We are about to move into sales forecasting. However we will revisit the issue of the statistical forecast when we move to Chapter 8: "Combining the Sales Forecast with the Statistical Forecast." At that point we run a similar type of competition that was run in this chapter, where we will do an analysis to answer the question: For what areas of the PLC database does including a sales forecast improve forecast accuracy, and in what cases does it not?

CHAPTER 6

Sales Forecasting

The best way to move a company in the right direction towards getting a quality sales forecast is to have a **quality statistical forecast**. Through testing it can be determined which PLCs require sales forecasting input, and which PLCs are better off with using statistical forecasting. This places the Sales/Marketing group into a superior position for providing their input, because they have fewer PLCs in which to provide input. A common mistake that companies make is to assume that sales forecasting can and should provide its **input to every PLC**. This is an inaccurate assumption based upon what we know about judgment methods, as many PLCs work better without sales input. Secondly, providing input to every PLC is draining for the Sales group, and with so many PLCs to update, often they will forget to update many of the PLCs assigned to them. A far more effective strategy is for Forecasting to perform the study that shows **which PLCs require sales input,** and then communicate this list to sales. When I have done this study and produced a short list of PLCs, usually Sales/Marketing is relieved when they see their reduced workload. Reducing the number of PLCs is actually a first step towards a more fruitful relationship between Sales/Marketing and Supply Chain Forecasting because Sales/Marketing is almost always appreciative of the reduction in workload. More emphasis can now be placed on those PLCs that can actually be improved with sales input and more time can be spent on a smaller number of items, which typically translates into better outcomes.

Effective forecasting departments are able to produce a forecast accuracy that is relatively close in its potential accuracy, and the manual forecast adjustments tend to be limited to those product or product-location combinations that actually benefit from adjustment.[1] It should be remembered that judgment forecasting methods, of which sales forecasting is one type, are expensive, and they are only intended to **augment** the statistical forecasting process. Judgment methods are not meant to be the dominant method used, except in situations where there are few items to be forecasted and statistical methods don't work very well. Computers, when fed correct demand history, can process and produce forecasts much less expensively than when judgment techniques are used, and therefore judgment techniques are typically reserved for highly valuable outcomes or for exceptions (i.e., a change that is not reflected in demand history.). This is explained well by the following quotation.

---

[1] Forecast accuracy potential is the desirable and achievable forecast accuracy, which is predicated on the environment. There is no **one** level of potential forecast accuracy. For instance, service parts have an irregular demand pattern. A service part demand history per month may look like the following:

Jan,	Feb,	Mar,	April,	May,	June,	July,	April
0	0	0	1	0	0	2	1

Imagine developing a forecasting algorithm that can predict this type of demand pattern. Under such a demand history, a high forecast accuracy using any forecasting mathematics is not possible, because there is no pattern to repeat. If one evaluates the environment at many companies, the actual consumption is more forecastable than the demand history. However, the stuffing and forecast promotions as well as a variety of other activities greatly reduces the potential forecast accuracy.

The objective of forecasting is not to attain a hypothetical or simply desirable forecast accuracy in the abstract accuracy level. Instead it is to attain something close to the forecast accuracy potential. Each further investment in forecasting capability may bring forecast accuracy improvement, but will also have a cost. This is explained in the following article.

http://www.scmfocus.com/demandplanning/2012/02/how-much-can-your-forecasting-accuracy-be-improved/

"The expensive, time-intensive nature of qualitative (aka judgment) forecasting is another reason (in addition to the bias caused by inconsistencies in judgment that occur in repetitive decision making) that qualitative forecasting techniques are unsuitable for generating large numbers of forecasts such as forecasting products by SKU and by location (SKUL)." – Sales Forecasting Management

However, this is exactly how many companies perform sales forecasting.

Considering Market Intelligence, Judgment Methods, and Bias

The argument has been presented to me that Sales/Marketing should be allowed to change (to forecast?) because of their domain expertise in marketing intelligence. However, companies rarely recognize the fact that in many studies, Sales/Marketing is known to have the **highest forecast bias of any contributor to the forecast**. The bias of Sales/Marketing in forecasting is so well known that the software vendor Right90 has developed its main application with a focus on managing the bias of sales forecasts. To provide a shorthand explanation, Right90's approach falls into the following steps:

1. *Step 1:* Recognize the historical research on sales forecast bias

2. *Step 2:* Measure forecast bias of each individual providing forecasting input

3. *Step 3:* Control this input:

   a. *Allow Good Input:* Let input with a history of improving the forecast through to change the forecast

   b. *Block Bad Input:* Prevent input with a history of decreasing forecast accuracy

What Right90 has essentially done is to develop software to more efficiently perform Steps 2 and 3. Right90 develops a four-factor measurement of any individual providing forecast input. (Of course, Step 1 would have occurred through the company making the decision to purchase and implement Right90.) This is called the "Trust Factor," and the criteria are accuracy, bias, consistency and completeness, as is shown in the screen shot below. Each individual forecaster is measured on these criteria.

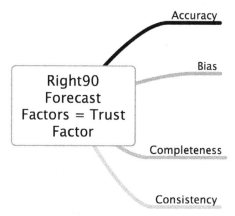

Here is how Right90 scores forecasts.

Personnel	Sales	QTD Actuals Q4 ' 10	My Target Q4 ' 10	LTG Q3'09	Trust Factor	Ac	Bi	Cp	Cn
Jason Dryer	$55,000.00	$29,500.00	$150,000.00	$120,500.00	2.5	3.7	-60%	2.0	3.0
Sandy Lewis	$200,000.00	$25,000.00	$150,000.00	$125,000.00	2.1	2.7	60%	4.0	2.0
Reggie Davidson	$150,000.00	$80,000.00	$150,000.00	$70,000.00	1.3	3.7	-55%	1.0	2.8
Bob Torrence	$180,000.00	$65,000.00	$150,000.00	$85,000.00	1.5	2.7	50%	2.0	4.0
Angela Rial	$190,000.00	$97,000.00	$150,000.00	$53,000.00	2.9	3.5	32%	1.0	2.5
Total	$775,000.00	$296,500.00	$750,000.00	$453,500.00	2.1	2.2	4.0%	2.0	3.2

Trust Worksheet — Return to Dashboard — Hide Tr Details — Elements of Trust

In Right90, each individual receives a rating. This rating influences how the forecast input is used to augment the statistical forecast in situations where a statistical forecast is used.

Right90's application is quite interesting and I would say unique because the vast majority of the market for enterprise forecasting software **is directed towards statistical forecasting,** something that Right90 themselves point out in their documentation.

> *"Unfortunately, most demand planning applications have been become 'algorithmic planning' applications that rely solely upon the algorithms to predict future demand. These applications have left out*

> *two critical inputs that reflect the most important view of demand:*
> *the customers' view of demand."*
>   – Put the S Back into Sales and Operations Planning

Some may think that the situation has improved with the broad adoption of CRM applications. However, Right90 explains how this is not the case.

> *"These applications are structured based on production hierarchies,*
> *not the sales or customer view of demand, and hence cannot integrate*
> *correctly with CRM applications. When data in the CRM system fails*
> *to integrate with data in the demand planning application, sales reps*
> *do not adopt the demand planning application."*
>   – Put the S Back into Sales and Operations Planning

This is why Right90 proposes that CRM be integrated to the statistical forecasting/demand planning system.

> *"Integrating into a CRM platform creates commonality and tight*
> *linkage between data sets. Recently closed and pipeline opportunities*
> *can be imported into a forecasting application upon which sales*
> *and revenue performance can be measured and managed. In such*
> *a system, sales forecast data is automatically shared with the*
> *CRM system, providing additional information linked to accounts,*
> *opportunities, sales regions, and markets."*
>   – From Misery to Mastery

This also creates a common platform that will allow for future integration of applications.

However as has been pointed out, effective forecasting environments have some type of filter and do not let **all** of the proposed forecast adjustments reach the forecast. Right90 regiments this process so that good and bad input can be measured and filtered in and away from the final forecast.

How Right90's Application Works
Right90's application allows an overseer to observe forecast accuracy in a con-

trolled environment, in which the input of the monitored parties input is recorded and clearly displayed.

In Right90, each individual receives a rating. This rating influences how the forecast input is used to augment the statistical forecast in situations where a statistical forecast is used.

However, I work for many clients where new software is not an option. While specific software can certainly make the process far more efficient, the same concept can be adopted without necessarily using this software—albeit with less efficiency than if an application like Right90 were purchased. This is a perfect activity for the role of the Forecasting Lead, a position that I will discuss at length further on in this book.

Right90 makes a specialized sales forecasting application, and proposes that this is an important application for any company that creates a sales forecast. I tend to agree. However, the fact is that many companies do not want to purchase a specialized sales forecasting application. Therefore, in these environments, the work that Right90 does within the application can be done with other, more simplified approaches.

Clarity on Bias

I have included the following quotation from my previous *book Supply Chain Forecasting Software*:

Forecast Bias Definition

> *"Forecast bias is a tendency for a forecast to be consistently higher or lower than the actual value. Forecast bias is distinct from forecast error in that a forecast can have any level of error but still be completely unbiased. For instance, even if a forecast is 15 percent higher than the actual values half the time and 15 percent lower than the actual values the other half of the time, it has no bias. But forecast which is on average 15 percent lower than the actual value has both a 15 percent error and a 15 percent bias. Bias can exist in statistical forecasting or in judgment methods. However, it is much more common with judgment methods and is in fact one of the major disadvantages with judgment methods. For judgment methods, bias can be conscious, in which case it is often driven by the institutional incentives provided to the forecaster. Bias can also be subconscious. A good example of subconscious bias is the optimism bias, which is a natural human characteristic."*

> – Supply Chain Forecasting Software

More on forecast bias can be read at the following article.

http://www.scmfocus.com/demandplanning/2012/02/forecastbias/

Regardless of the forecasting environment (supply chain and non-supply chain), bias is a constant factor in forecasting, yet not all that much has been written about it (at least compared to the challenge it presents). Few authors are willing to see the forecast bias inherent in judgment methods as anything beyond a cognitive bias (that is, an unconscious bias or an error in cognition) and most often companies do not focus on removing forecast bias, as explained in the following article.

http://www.scmfocus.com/demandplanning/2010/07/why-do-companies-re-fuse-to-remove-forecast-bias/

Specific Bias Issues

At many companies, Sales/Marketing is considered to have the right domain expertise for forecasting (they understand the products, their customers, and the market). However, their incentives, what these incentives mean for bias, and how this bias might affect the forecast adjustments that they make, are often not accounted for in the management of their input.[2] As pointed out by Right90, many companies are strongly disinclined hear bad news that might mean lower sales.

> *"Most executives are conflicted. On one hand, they need and want to know what is going to happen as far in advance as possible with enough detail to understand the impact to the business. On the other hand, they want that outcome to be positive and hate to hear bad news. Some are able to differentiate between these two needs and actually reward sales people for honesty, even if that produces news they do not want to hear ("don't shoot the messenger"). These companies tend to have sales forecasts that are much more accurate and timely than other companies.*

---

[2] Forecast bias is not a matter of education, and does not improve due to education level, although mistakenly it is often thought to improve. An excellent example of this is the pharmaceutical story of Prilosec versus Nexium. Nexium is a copycat drug that was developed by AstraZeneca. Nexium is actually a slight alteration to the chemical compound referred to as Prilosec. This alteration was made because Prilosec was coming off of its patent, and AstraZeneca stood to lose a large market. Prior to Prilosec's patent expiring, AstraZeneca compensated doctors and distributed false information that Nexium was a better drug. To facilitate a switch to Nexium before the patent expired, they reduced the price of Nexium so that it was lower than Prilosec. The program was a "success," with many patients transferred to an expensive drug when an almost chemically identical drug was available as a generic. The physicians who participated in this scheme had a bias: they were compensated for making the switch against their patients' financial interests (although not health interest as there the drugs are copies of one another). One of the most problematic issues is when bias is not acknowledged. The vast majority of patients were not aware that AstraZeneca compensated physicians; they thought they were getting an honest medical opinion. Example after example demonstrates that bias will affect recommendations and predictions no matter how educated the individual. In fact highly educated individuals have an even more dangerous interaction with bias, because they can claim superior domain expertise.

Others tell sales people that if they cannot make a forecast they want to hear, the salesperson needs to find another job. They assume that if they allow sales people to tell them anything other than the answer they want to hear, that the sales people will assume they have a license to miss their number. This is not necessarily true and often results in a dangerous situation where the sales reps are only telling management what they want to hear. In situations like these, when the sales people can't make their numbers, they say that everything is okay while they line up their next jobs and make excuses for short term performance ('that deal is just two quarters away…'). This produces a classic 'house of cards' effect in the sales forecast and can be especially catastrophic when there is a dramatic turn or change in the market. Many companies experience huge forecast surprises in these situations."

— 7 Secrets of Sales Forecasting

Obviously, when people's jobs depend upon their forecast being high, this is a prescription for forecast bias. Some very public and extreme examples of forecast bias come to us from Wall Street. While Wall Street firms create all types of forecasts, they often have a financial bias in the forecast becoming reality. For instance, when Goldman Sachs produces a buy rating for a financial instrument, they do not declare whether or not they currently own any of the instruments (usually they have some type of position in the items they are forecasting). Their position as a respected source of information on the topic of finance allows them to promote instruments they already own. For some reason, it's very unusual for media outlets to question whether Goldman Sachs should declare their financial position with regards to the forecast. Instead the forecast is simply repeated as if Goldman Sachs is some unbiased entity that just wants to get its forecasts out to help people make better decisions. I use Goldmand Sacks as an example, but in fact this lack of disclosure is the rule in the financial services industry.

Converting Market Intelligence into Forecast Adjustments

It is important to appraise the following factors with respect to how market intelligence is converted into forecasting input:

1. *The Quality of Market Intelligence:* Each person in Sales/Marketing that has a domain expertise of market intelligence is a potential source of information about the market that can be used to create forecast adjustments. Market intelligence can be rated on a continuum from high quality to low quality.

2. *Technical Skills:* Knowledge of how to convert the market intelligence into adjustments, which can include both the process understanding and the technical skills.

3. *Conversion Tools:* The specific tools that Sales/Marketing has to apply their domain experience.

4. *Time Allocated for Forecasting:* It's common for Sales/Marketing individuals to complain that they do not have the time to make all the forecast adjustments required, as my project experience and this following quotation attests.[3]

---

[3] The degree to which Sales/Marketing dislike forecasting is expressed quite nicely by this quotation.

> *"Anyone in sales understands the time-tested ritual of the Monday morning sales call. Typically, the call goes smoothly and everyone is excited about the week ahead, the progress being made at key accounts, and the promise of closing several significant deals. Then suddenly those dreaded words are spoken, 'Forecasts are due this Friday" triggering a collective sigh from attendees on the call. The energy built in the first 58 minutes of the call is quickly deflated in the final 2. While we all understand that updating forecasts is an important process on the road to hitting company revenue targets, it can be one of those exercises that most would readily admit they would rather not undertake.*
>
> *Forecasting is not met with such disdain because of what it is, but because of how it is done. The painstaking process of collecting updates from reps spread out across the country or the globe; consolidating forecasts into a single report that sales executives, finance executives, and others can understand; and communicating changes and how they have an impact on the company's revenue targets is not for the faint of heart. Most often the sales forecast, once compiled, is already out of date and not very useful for the intended stakeholders."*
>
> – Misery to Mastery

"Often forecasting is viewed by Sales as extra work preventing them from selling."
  – 5 Best Practices to Develop a Trusted, Actionable Forecast.

If Sales/Marketing does not have adequate amounts of time to apply the market intelligence to the PLCs, then one can expect the comprehensiveness of the input to decline.

As should be clear, it is insufficient to simply declare that Sales/Marketing should make many forecast adjustments because they are "closest to the customers." A better way of managing the input for forecast adjustments from Sales/Marketing is to evaluate the above four factors and to ensure that they match with the requirements for forecast adjustments.

The Incentives of Sales/Marketing

Sales and Marketing are primarily evaluated and compensated based upon sales. Generally speaking, forecast accuracy is **not** included in their incentives. In cases where measurements of the forecast accuracy of sales or marketing are taken and discussed (for instance, in consensus forecasting meetings), this measurement rarely has any implication for their compensation or yearly reviews. Therefore, when I analyze the forecasting error at companies, it's quite common for the forecast to have a positive bias. Positive bias can be introduced by either the statistical forecasting system or by the Sales/Marketing input. However, in my forecast error analyses it is normally significantly larger in the Sales/Marketing forecast.

I have one interesting story in this regard. When speaking with a group of marketers at a company, I learned that they were to be measured on forecast accuracy, but this idea was shelved when none of the marketers could meet a forecast accuracy of 60 percent of the stated target at the beginning of the year. Some individuals in Sales/Marketing seem to debate that they are measured by forecast accuracy, but once we get into the details it turns out that that they believe they are measured this way because there may have been discussion within the company about possibly adding a forecast accuracy measurement to the other Sales/Marketing measurements. It should be noted that discussion about doing something is not the same as actually <u>doing</u> something. One should not propose they are measured by some KPI when it has never progressed past the discussion phase.

However, the problem is, no matter if Sales or Marketing were to put an individual measurement emphasis on forecast accuracy, the emphasis would not be sufficient to counteract the effects of forecast bias **of the other** sales measurements. At most companies, the management within Sales and Marketing does not **value** forecast accuracy as highly as they value sales goals.[4] Often this point is missed by many in Supply Chain who think that Sales/Marketing should be measured on the basis of forecast error. This leads to the question of: who should actually be making the forecast adjustments and who should be simply providing input on adjustments? I will explore this point in detail further on in this book.

Quite naturally, measuring individuals on sales volume without measuring them on inventory or forecast accuracy will promote the inclination to **over forecast; that is to deliberately pad the forecast above what one thinks the sales level will actually be**. Over forecasting provides the ability to meet a higher sales volume with service level and sales volume.[5] Over forecasting is so common in this scenario that its technical name is "hedging," which is...

> *"Used so that 'the factory will have stuff when I want it.' This game may be played by salespersons or customers, especially when capacity is tight or for new products." – Sales Forecast "Game Playing"*
> – Why It's Bad and What You Can Do About It

---

[4] This issue comes down to not differentiating between forecasting and business planning. *"Sales forecasting can be used to facilitate business planning, but this outcome cannot occur if sales forecasts are forced to agree with independently generated revenue targets in the business plan."* – Sales Forecasting Management

[5] It is interesting because I have discussed this with some sales and marketing groups and they often stated that they were "indirectly" incentivized to build stock – but "not directly." However, this is not true. Actually, they are **directly** incentivized to build stock. High forecasts lead to higher stock, which leads to higher in-stock levels for their products. The relationship is quite direct. To accept the notion that there is only an indirect incentive to build stock would be to not acknowledge the very obvious connection between forecasting and inventory building.

Companies can carry a limited amount of inventory; any overage of inventory will naturally come at the expense of other products managed by other Sales/Marketing resources. While it may seem so from the outside, it should be understood that Sales/Marketing is not some big happy family with unified objectives. In Sales, the salespeople are competing with each other – and this competition goes beyond who get the biggest bonus. If one salesperson can have capacity allocated to their products and can take capacity from another salesperson, usually they will do it. Each salesperson is paid a bonus on their sales (normally), not on the sales of other salespeople. Furthermore, salespeople often have aggressive goals, and meeting those goals not only means a bonus, but can mean the difference between keeping a job and losing a job. In Marketing similar issues exist. For instance, one group in Marketing may have an incentive to have its promotions supported with a high availability of stock, which may mean reducing the in-stock position for other products. However, this particular marketing group may only be measured on the effect of the promotion for particular promoted products.

Another important point to consider is that Sales and Marketing are **not measured** on whether or not they keep inventories low. This is why Sales/Marketing routinely set such unsupportable inventory and service levels. For instance, it is very common for sales groups to target 99 percent service levels for most of its products. However, except for the items with the highest profitability, normally this service level is not sustainable because the inventory rises so dramatically at service levels above 95 percent. In every case I have checked, companies do not achieve these very high service levels because of how they measure the service level. There are many ways to manipulate the service level to make it look better than it actually is. One of the most common is the backorder. If a product is out of stock, it is placed on backorder, which means it does not count against the service level.[6]

---

[6] Service levels need to be set not in the abstract, but with an understanding of the benefits as well as the costs of the attained service level. It is irrational to set service levels without this appreciation—and based upon platitudes that bring up the "importance" of service levels. Some products compete on price, and in those cases, it is understood that service levels cannot be expected to be the same than if the product is higher margin.

In most cases, service levels should not be set to maximize sales, but to maximize prof-

Inventory level is a KPI[7] for which Supply Chain is measured. Inventory goals and sales goals are contradictory and it does not make sense to have one group held accountable for one of the goals, and another group held accountable for the other. At many companies, the end result of all of this is that Supply Chain does not control a **major input regarding how it is measured**. Even if one knew nothing about these companies, it would be relatively easy to predict that this would result in a situation where one group understands that they are held accountable for a series of KPIs that are driven by another KPI they do not control. This is a perfect scenario to create tension between two groups.

Forecasting on Goals or Based Upon Pressure Rather than Likelihoods

In discussing the new product introduction forecasts with Sales and Marketing, I consistently receive the feedback that Sales and Marketing are expected to develop forecasts based upon what the company would "like to sell."

Let's say that an overall market for a particular type of tuna fish is $1,000,000 per month. If the company were to decide to offer that type of tuna fish, it may be considered desirable to attain a 20 percent market share. Sales or Marketing may then submit a forecast of $200,000 of tuna fish per month.

However, this is a sales goal; **it is not a forecast.** There is nothing wrong with having a goal of achieving a 20 percent market share, but until there is more evidence that the goal will be achieved, it makes little sense to **stock** to the goal.[8] This difference between a sales goal and a forecast is often lost on Sales

---

its. This is why service levels should not be set by Sales or Marketing because of their tendency to set maximum service levels that are centered around their personal performance incentives. Unfortunately that is how service levels are often set in companies, with Supply Chain being tasked with achieving unrealistic service level goals.

Service levels can actually be determined by other values, as explained at the following link: http://www.scmfocus.com/3s/

[7] Key Performance Indicator

[8] This is defined in the literature on sales forecasting as *"Enforcing: Maintaining a higher forecast than actually anticipated in order to keep forecasts **in line with the sales or financial goals of the organization,** such as 'making the quarter.' Used when 'taking*

because in Sales the goal is the forecast. That is, Sales uses the term "forecast" to mean something different than what the term means in most other areas, including Supply Chain.

Let's review a definition of sales forecasting to drive this point home:

> *"Sales as a management function, typically is concerned with setting goals for the individual members of the sales force and motivating those salespeople to exceed those goals. The common factor in the sales forecasting level for the sales function is the product, for this is what a salesperson is rewarded for selling."*
> – Sales Forecast Management

One can see the problem right off the bat. If the sales force is motivated and evaluated on how they exceed the forecast, then they will have an incentive to under-forecast. After all, the best way to achieve one's goal is to make the goal easier to achieve. Supply Chain, on the other hand, does not strive to exceed the forecast, because it would mean consumption of safety stock, or a stock out. Supply Chain hopes the actual sales are as close to the forecast as possible.

A forecast is one's estimate of what the demand will be, and it should have no intersection with what one would **like** the demand to be. This would be like asking a person whether or not his or her favorite team will win the game. One can expect a biased response. In fact, forecast bias is introduced into the process simply by the selection of a biased forecaster.

Inaccurate and Inconsistent Forecast Adjustments from Sales

Based on even a discussions with Sales and Marketing (in a variety of companies), it is quite evident that the means by which Sales tends to make forecast adjustments does not leverage a number of techniques that are designed to make adjustments more consistent and scientific. I've made the following observations during discussions with Sales and Marketing at a number of com-

---

the number down is not acceptable.'" - http://forecasters.org/foresight/wp/wp-content/uploads/Forecast_Game_Playing_Mello_OSU_IIF_13.pdf

panies:

- *A Lack of Quantification and Measurement:* If we take the example of adjusting for promotions, Sales and Marketing often use "feel" in order to determine how much of an increase or decrease to provide to the forecast. Therefore, when a promotional adjustment is made, the management of these companies should **not have** confidence that it will be consistent with previous adjustments. The following quotation attests to this: *"It is hard to get a clear picture of what is good and what is not good in the forecast. Sales leaders are compelled to use estimation, intuition and guesswork to access the quality of the forecast and identify areas of risk."* – Removing Risk from Your Sales Forecast

- *Unaided Domain Expertise:* Essentially, many companies rely entirely on the concept of Sales and their market intelligence expertise to improve the statistical forecast, but without providing Sales and Marketing with the tools or with the support necessary to **apply** that domain expertise consistently.

- *Time Consuming Endeavors:* Because of the lack of tools and support provided to Sales and Marketing, they often rely upon market research (anything from counting competitor stock in retailers to performing market share analysis) to determine new product forecasts. Market research of this type turns out to be the most expensive type of forecasting effort in which one can engage—and it should be questioned as to whether this activity is necessary. Most companies already have similar products that could in many cases be leveraged (with some factors applied), allowing forecasts to be developed much more quickly.

Why Sales and Marketing Have So Much Control Over the Forecast at Many Companies

A clear lesson emerges from a lengthy analysis of forecasting history in fields ranging from supply chain forecasting to financial service forecasting. Extremely high levels of domain expertise—when combined with financial incentives that promote a bias—**do not result** in accurate forecasts. In fact, in the majority of cases it is quite the opposite. Loosely translated, having domain expertise **is not enough**. In fact, even if the domain expertise within Sales and

Marketing were excellent, at least three other elements necessary to produce a quality forecast would be missing. These elements are:

1. *Bias Control*

2. *Tools and Application Expertise*

3. *Statistical Forecast Accuracy*: With an improved statistical forecast, Sales/Marketing gets back a very important commodity: time. The number of PLC forecasts Sales/Marketing would be required to adjust declines steeply, and Sales/Marketing can focus the limited time they do have on the products that require their domain expertise.

Improving Sales/Marketing Forecasts

At many companies, Sales has a problematic combination of the following factors.

1. *Forecast Control:* A strong ability to perform forecast adjustment.

2. *Lack of Forecast Responsibility:* Incentives that are not tied to forecast accuracy, but other incentives that promote over forecasting.

These problems are not difficult to solve, as long as the interest and motivation exists to solve them. The reason many companies find themselves in this position is that they have not designed their incentives, control, and responsibilities in a way that is directed towards improving forecast accuracy. In fact, what are the incentives for forecast accuracy versus the incentives for sales and marketing? If Sales and Marketing sell more, they often receive financial bonuses (of course this applies more to Sales than Marketing). Forecast accuracy is typically not incentivized this way, even among those who work in forecasting.

There are two basic options that would address the forecast bias of Sales/Marketing.

1. *Option 1 – The Decentralized Approach*: Sales/Marketing could be measured and compensated partially on forecast accuracy, and continue to be allowed to change the forecast as they can now.

2. *Option 2 – The Centralized Approach*: Sales could provide forecast input, but how this input is used would be outside of their control.

The first option is more complicated to implement and would require more change, and more debate involving lengthy discussions on the details of "how" Sales/Marketing would be measured and compensated, etc. It is also riskier than the second option, and continues to force Sales/Marketing into doing something they would generally **prefer to spend less time doing.** An important rule of forecasting is that one should not rely on forecasts from those who are not particularly interested in forecasting, or are too busy to provide a thoroughly researched forecast. It is better to gather input from these individuals rather than to expect a usable forecast from them. For all of these reasons and more, I consider the second option to have a higher potential for better forecast outcomes.

One way or another, Sales/Marketing needs guidance on forecasting, and this is not only my opinion. In interviews at many companies, sales and marketing individuals have said this to me as well. I can also provide multiple examples of how the methods that Sales/Marketing use to come up with forecast adjustments are far behind approaches that I have used for some time. This forecast guidance must come from someone knowledgeable in both standard forecasting, forecasting software, as well as how to incorporate sales forecasting into the overall forecasting process. Every company should have a Forecasting Lead whose responsibility it is to help the Sales/Marketing forecasters to bring their input into the forecasting process in a controlled way. The Forecasting Lead develops the tools that would allow mathematical relationships to be developed that in turn would allow Sales/Marketing forecasters to provide their market intelligence input, and for the Forecasting Lead to **"translate"** that piece of information into adjustments to the statistical forecast. In order to explain how this would work for one example of a supported process, let us discuss how promotions forecasting would be affected by the addition of a Forecasting Lead.

The Role of the Forecasting Lead
Performing the tasks that I have described in this chapter—and doing them consistently—takes someone who is **focused** on these tasks and who knows

exactly how the system will respond to promotional and other manual forecast adjustments. This type of precision **can only be achieved** by a person whose primary focus and primary area of expertise is in this area. In fact, this is a point that is worthy of elaboration.

There is an assumption that Sales/Marketing can provide good quality input to the forecast without assistance. Let us analyze that assumption for a moment. Imagine that Sales/Marketing is trained to use the forecasting system. Could a group that has a sales bias, comprised of people with different backgrounds and skill sets than a professional forecaster, outperform a scenario where Sales/Marketing simply provides input to a Forecasting Lead who then creates the forecast? My experience tells me this is highly doubtful. In addition to my anecdotes that lead me to this conclusion, a key observation by those

Forecast Accuracy Dashboard

	Accuracy	Bias	Action
Statistical Forecast	66%	-5%	
Manual (Total) Forecast	72%	10%	
Sales Group 1	45%	15%	Use input sparingly - forecast input has low accuracy.
Sales Group 2	76%	4%	Use input, forecast accuracy is higher than statistical forecast.
Tom Jackson	35%	20%	Do not use forecast input from Tom Jackson
Don Hemmingway	87%	3%	Always use input from Don Hemmingway
Wal Mart	60%	-5%	Bring up forecast input from Wal Mart - use input sparingly.
Safeway	45%	-7%	Use input sparingly - forecast input has low accuracy.

who specialize in managing sales forecasts is that all sales forecasting processes **must** be intermediated. This key observation is at the root of the Right90 application. There may be two areas where the Sales/Marketing forecast is reviewed. The first may be within Sales and Marketing itself. An individual may be assigned to adjust the forecasts before they are sent to Supply Chain. Just as with Right90, this individual would adjust the forecasts often using the historical performance of each individual forecaster.

This forecast accuracy dashboard can be used by any individual who reviews the forecasts of a group. Forecasts can be adjusted based upon their historical forecast accuracy. The notion that the more forecasts that one receives the better (the" more the merrier" concept) does not work in forecasting because some inputs are superior to other; using the high quality forecasts and rejecting or de-emphasizing the inputs with low forecast accuracy can improve forecast accuracy. In this example above, forecasts from internal as well as external sources can be reviewed. It is just as important to track for internal forecasts as external. For instance, it is often considered virtuous to use the forecasts from customers, but frequently customers provide low quality forecasts. It makes the most sense to accept high quality forecasts from customers and stop using, or even stop receiving, low quality forecasts. For instance, there may be little reason to use forecasts from Safeway, as their forecast accuracy shown in the screen shot above is low. However, Safeway may have a low forecast accuracy for most of its products, but may in fact be able to forecast some products quite well. In this case, just part of the forecast from Safeway might be used. A big part of improving forecast accuracy, one that is greatly underemphasized as a technique, is to measure the forecast accuracy inputs that work, regardless of their source and to use those inputs over other inputs.

Once the forecasts have been intermediated from within Sales and Marketing, it usually makes sense to intermediate them again before they are used by Supply Chain. Of course the more the forecasts are reviewed within these groups, the less work Supply Chain has to do. However, it is common for forecasts from Sales/Marketing to flow into Supply Chain without any intermediation.

The Forecasting Lead is positioned to serve as a reviewer of the forecast that comes from Sales and Marketing. The Forecasting Lead is located in Supply Chain and is tasked with both improving the statistical forecasting output as well as working with Sales/Marketing to get their forecasting input into the statistical forecast.

1. *Forward Looking Adjustments:* The Forecasting Lead takes the Sales/Marketing domain expertise in market intelligence and applies the right changes to a system in order to adjust the forecast very precisely.

2. *Rearward Looking Adjustments:* The Forecasting Lead records previous features of the demand history (such as promotions) so that the demand history is ready to be used by the statistical forecasting methods.

This labor specialization not only improves the forecast accuracy, but improves the utilization of time for everyone involved in the forecasting process as well as those who sit downstream of the forecast, such as Supply Chain. Although improvements in forecast accuracy benefit so many processes downstream of forecasting, it is very difficult to fully quantify all of the benefits. Because of this, it is difficult to get funding approval for forecast improvement projects. Benefits such as reduced stock-outs and lower inventory are far easier to quantify; however the difficulty in quantifying other benefits means that forecasting improvement projects tend to be underfunded. It also means that many forecast improvement projects that could easily pay for themselves never get funded. Presently, it is quite common for various members of Supply Chain to second guess the forecast and make their own adjustments because they do not trust the forecast. An improved forecast can improve the time utilization of a very large number of employees.

Conclusion

The best way to move a company in the right direction towards getting a quality sales forecast is to have a quality statistical forecast. Reducing the number of PLCs is actually a first step towards a more fruitful relationship between Sales/Marketing and Supply Chain Forecasting because Sales/Marketing is almost always appreciative of the reduction in workload. Effective forecasting departments are able to produce a forecast accuracy that is relatively close in its potential accuracy, and the manual forecast adjustments tend to be limited to those product or product-location combinations that actually benefit from adjustment. Judgment method – of which sales forecasting is one type, is expensive. Judgment methods are not meant to be the dominant method used, except in situations where there are few items to be forecasted and statistical methods don't work very well. Computers, when fed correct demand history, can process and produce forecasts much less expensively than when judgment techniques are used, and therefore judgment techniques are typically reserved for highly valuable outcomes or for exceptions (i.e., a change that is not reflected in demand history.) Right90 is one of the few applications to focus exclusively on the sales forecast. Right90's application allows an overseer to observe forecast accuracy in a controlled environment, in which the input of the monitored parties input is recorded and clearly displayed.

Another important point to consider is that Sales and Marketing are **not measured** on whether or not they keep inventories low. This is why Sales/Marketing routinely set such unsupportable inventory and service levels. For instance, it is very common for sales groups to target 99 percent service levels for most of its products. However, except for the items with the highest profitability, normally this service level is not sustainable because the inventory rises so dramatically at service levels above 95 percent. In every case I have checked, companies do not achieve these very high service levels because of how they measure the service level. There are many ways to manipulate the service level to make it look better than it actually is.

There is an assumption that Sales/Marketing can provide good quality input to the forecast without assistance. Let us analyze that assumption for a moment. Imagine that Sales/Marketing is trained to use the forecasting system. Could a group that has a sales bias, comprised of people with different backgrounds and skill sets than a professional forecaster, outperform a scenario where Sales/Marketing simply provides input to a Forecasting Lead who then creates the forecast? My experience tells me this is highly doubtful. In addition to my anecdotes that lead me to this conclusion, a key observation by those who specialize in managing sales forecasts is that all sales forecasting processes **must** be intermediated.

CHAPTER 7

The Sales Forecast and CRM

CRM (customer relationship management) is one of the fastest growing categories of enterprise software. Forbes predicts that in 2015 the sales of CRM will surpass that of ERP, which will be the first time that ERP will be in second place in the enterprise market since the mid-1980s. Although CRM continues to be a very popular application, the results of a review of CRM implementations in companies can often be quite uninspiring. I have sat with a number of marketing and sales people, reviewing the data in the company's CRM system only to find that the input is incomplete. The session typically ends with the sales or marketing resource saying something like *"we really need to get on our people to start completing more information."*

CRM really started as a contact management system and has since grown in a number of directions. In fact, CRM often has so many different attributes that it can be difficult to say definitively what CRM actually is. For instance, there is another enterprise software category called customer engagement software (one example of this being Marketo) that has overlap with CRM. Therefore, while CRM was never developed for forecasting, it is often presumed that it is used for forecasting. In fact, many CRM software vendors propose that their system is the key to improving the accuracy of the sales forecast. This is a complaint on the part of Right90; many times they will be told by prospects that sales forecasting is taken care of because they have a CRM system. A major problem is that CRM is **not designed** to track the sales at a product-location combination. Instead, the unit of measure of CRM applications tends to be sales and the focus is on the customer.

Here we can see the pipeline report within BaseCRM. Notice that this reports on the revenue. Usually the salesperson is not going to type in what was purchased by the customer. BaseCRM refers this to as a Sales Funnel Report. However, it is not a report that can be used to improve the forecast at the product-location combination.

Here is a quote from the BaseCRM white paper *5 Reports Every VP of Sales Should Master.*

> "When you pull the sales funnel analysis report you see the hard
> numbers of your team's activity over a given timeframe. You see how
> many deals came in, how many were qualified and what happened
> from there. And here's where the real perk of this report comes in—
> you can see where your team stands and pinpoint where they need

coaching. The sales funnel report calculates conversions at every milestone along your sales process and this is insight you will use well beyond your Monday meeting. Sales funnel analysis conversion reporting breaks down into percentages of how many leads qualified, how many qualified leads were given a quote, how many quotes moved into the contract phase and how many contracts were won. With this data you can identify strengths and weaknesses in your lead generation and sales processes."

These are all valuable things for sales, but again they do not help improve the supply chain forecast.

Here we can see the Incoming Deals report within BaseCRM. Notice that this reports on the revenue. Two salespeople are compared to each other on the basis of sales revenue. This report is great for tracking salespeople, but not useful for improving the statistical forecast.

Notice the further quote from BaseCRM on how tracking the incoming deals or pipeline is beneficial:

> *"Using a simple sales pipeline will help you track sales, visualize leads, and organize your follow-ups. And, most importantly, a sales pipeline will give your business a wealth of information like why deals are won or lost, where your leads come from, and how your leads translate to sales. This is critical information that will help improve your sales process and help you win more deals. Using a sales pipeline is the first step towards making you and your team 10x more productive."*
>
> – Understanding Your Pipeline and Sales Tracking

According to the BaseCRM marketing collateral, effective sales analytics tracks the prospect through the following stages:

1. Prospecting

2. Qualified

3. Quote

4. Closure

5. Won/Lost

Furthermore the sales team should be able to categorize the reasons for the lost sale.

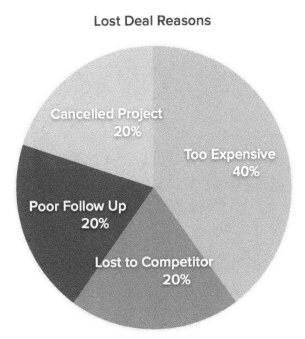

By categorizing the reason the prospect did not buy, the sales team can adjust their strategy the next time around.

Here is a sales funnel analysis provided by BaseCRM.

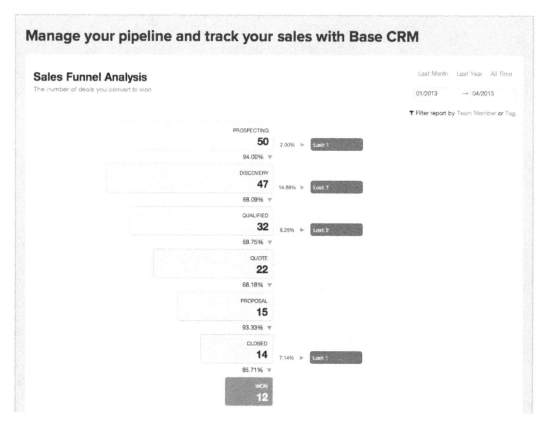

Notice how aggregated this report is. Furthermore, the only part of this report that would be of interest to generating the final forecast would be the number of sales won. All the information prior to this is exclusively for Sales. Information on what is planned to be sold is interesting and useful to Supply Chain for the purpose of creating the final forecast. And even this is only interesting to Supply Chain at the specific PLC level.

This report shows how each salesperson is progressing against their goals. Once again, notice that revenues are the focus of the report.

BaseCRM even has a Sales Forecast screen, so let's take a look at that report.

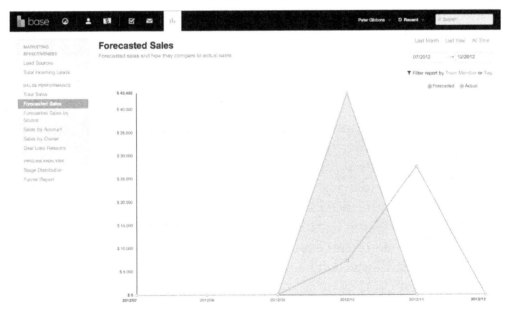

This again shows revenue, in this case forecasted revenue versus actual revenue. If you look towards the left, you can see that the sales can be viewed by source, by account, and by owner. This allows the salesperson to adjust their concentration.

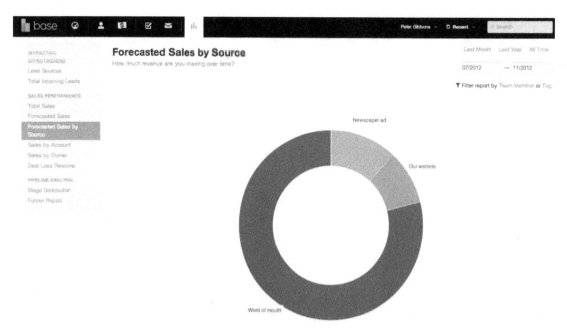

This report again shows revenue, and perhaps by looking at this report the salesperson can decide to focus more on newspaper ads. Perhaps this salesperson's sales are low from newspapers compared to other salespeople, or compared to previous months. This report can prompt the salesperson to discuss with marketing whether newspaper ads are running the same way they did previously.

Conclusion

While CRM was never developed for forecasting, it is often presumed that it is used for forecasting. In fact, many CRM software vendors propose that their system is the key to improving the accuracy of the sales forecast. CRM is focused almost exclusively on revenue tracking and forecasting rather than forecasting a particular product-location combination. BaseCRM was used as an example CRM system in this chapter. This is not a criticism of BaseCRM, which I consider one of the best CRM systems; instead it is a feature of how CRM systems are designed. The answer to better sales forecasting is not going to be found in the CRM system.

CHAPTER 8

Combining Sales Forecast with Statistical Forecasting

Just about every company must combine their sales forecast with their statistical forecast, but even so, few companies research the proven ways to perform this combination. A comprehensive meta-analysis of forty-seven studies into how to combine judgment forecasting (of which sales is a subcategory) and statistical forecasting was performed by J Scott Armstrong and Fred Collopy. A meta-analysis combines and compares multiple analyses. It is a way of coming to a conclusion as to what the combined insights are on any particular researched topic.[1]

The following lists some interesting observations from this meta-analysis. This list is a bit long, but many important insights are included in this paper. I have included points relevant to some of the insights in parenthesis.

- This literature suggests that integration of judgment and statistical forecasts generally improves accuracy when the experts have domain knowledge and when significant trends are

---

[1] http://en.wikipedia.org/wiki/Meta-analysis

involved. (This means that it is beneficial to add judgment methods—which would be input from Sales or Marketing— to statistical forecasting when there are "significant" changes to the environment and when the experts actually have domain knowledge. By inference, if either of these two preconditions is missing, the input may not improve forecast accuracy. This is an important observation and it should be considered cautionary to those who would assume that judgment methods always improve forecast accuracy.)

- Integration (of judgment/Sales/Marketing forecasting and statistical forecasting) harms accuracy when judgment is biased or its use is unstructured.

- Judgment is useful because domain experts often have knowledge of recent events, the effects of which have **not yet been observed** in a time series, of events that have occurred in the past but are not expected to recur in the future, or of events that have not occurred in the past but are expected for the future.

- Experts may see more in the data than is warranted. And they are subject to a variety of biases such as anchoring, double counting, and optimism.

- Integration of judgment and statistical methods can lead to substantial gains in accuracy under certain conditions (in comparison to using either of them alone). But when incorrectly applied, **as often happens**, integration can harm accuracy. (This is an interesting observation that generalizes to Sales/Marketing and statistical forecasting; it is a certainty that many companies that combine their Sales/Marketing and statistical forecast actually reduce their forecast accuracy.)

- It seems to be a common belief that the more information experts have about a series, the better judgmental forecasts they will be able to make. However, laboratory studies have concluded that additional information can harm accuracy. Further, in some circumstances at least, confidence grows even as accuracy declines (e.g., Davis, Lohse & Kottemann 1994). (This points to the diminishing marginal utility after a certain point, of using multiple information sources. It is very common on forecasting projects to hear, "If we only had access to this information from A or B, our forecast would be even better." However, that is not necessarily true.)

- If one could know which method—statistical or judgmental—would produce the more accurate forecast, then that **method should probably be used, or at least weighed more heavily**. In practice, alternative forecasts nearly always contain some added information. (This exact approach is laid out in this book.)

- Revision does not appear to be the most effective way to use judgment. It is distressing that software developers have been making it easier for forecasters to make unstructured judgmental adjustments. Instead, software should encourage prior inputs of judgment and inform how to structure this information. The evaluation should compare the accuracy of the forecasts with and without the revisions. (This is an important observation that goes to a topic that was discussed earlier: who makes the forecast adjustment? What has been proposed earlier is that the Forecasting Lead makes the adjustment based upon the Sales/Marketing forecast. This is a structured way of making changes.)

The approach laid out in this book is entirely consistent with the above research. I had already come to many of the same conclusions before reading this meta research, and luckily the method I developed dovetailed with the conclusions of this meta research, in particular, the observation that whatever produces a more accurate forecast should be used or weighted more heavily. This is the very foundation of the approach presented in this book.

Paul Goodwin, in the *International Journal of Forecasting*, brought up another very important research conclusion upon which this book is based.

> *"A similar study by Lim and O'Connor also found that forecasters tended to underweight statistical forecasts in favor of their own judgments, even when attention was drawn to the superior accuracy of the statistical forecast."*

This evidence supports my conclusion (which I determined through observation on my projects): Sales/Marketing should provide input to the forecast, but should not be making the changes directly to the final forecast. Of course this does not mean they cannot use a forecasting or CRM system to enter their forecasts, but the way this data flows to the final forecast should be mediated. However, as the reason for the change to the statistically produced forecast must be explained to the intermediary in any case, it makes even more sense for the Sales/Marketing forecasts to come with an explanation that shares the market intelligence with the forecasting intermediary—what I refer to as the Forecasting Lead.

Our Approach to Combining Sales with Statistical Forecasting

The same approach outlined in Chapter 5: "Comparing Best Fit Forecasting to Homegrown Statistical Forecasting Models" should be followed to combine the sales and statistical forecast. The forecast history of each **should be tested**, and then the PLC database segmented for which approach works best for each PLC. The logic of this looks like the following:

Flow and Logic of Combining Forecasts

		Overall PLC Database			
Test 1	Best Fit VS. Homegrown	Best Fit > Homegrown		Homegrown > Best Fit	
Test 2	Statistical VS. Sales	Statistical > Sales	Sales > Statistical	Statistical > Sales	Sales > Statistical

This shows how testing the PLC database is assigned to different segments. After this is done, it is important to actually add these attributes to the database so those performing forecasting know how the specific PLC should be treated.

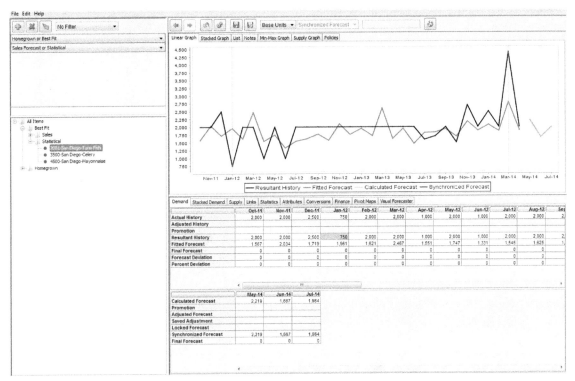

After the PLC database has been tested, I have taken the categories and created attributes that I have loaded into the forecasting system, making the analysis available right within the forecasting system. Notice the attributes to the left. I have categorized PLCs under Best Fit and Homegrown. Below that I have indicated whether the PLC is Sales (forecasted) or Statistical (forecasted). If I select the PLCs under Best Fit and Statistical, I find Tuna Fish at San Diego, Celery at San Diego, and Mayonnaise at San Diego.

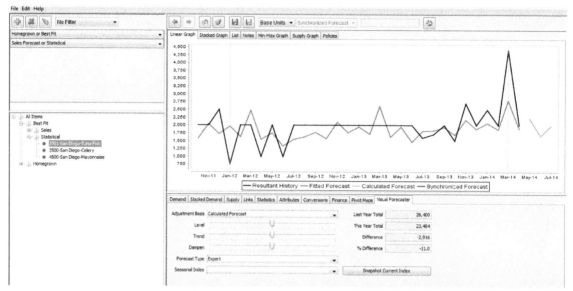

Because a best fit forecast is the best forecasting method for these PLCs, I have the "Expert" forecast type selected. In this application, Expert means best fit.

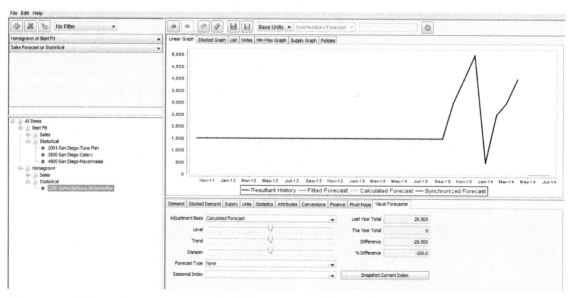

However, if I navigate over to the Homegrown hierarchy and then to the Statistical sub node, we can see the forecast type is set to None because here the homegrown forecast model (which is outside of this system) is used. Instead we would either perform forecasting for these PLCs outside of this system, or upload the forecast from the homegrown system to this system.

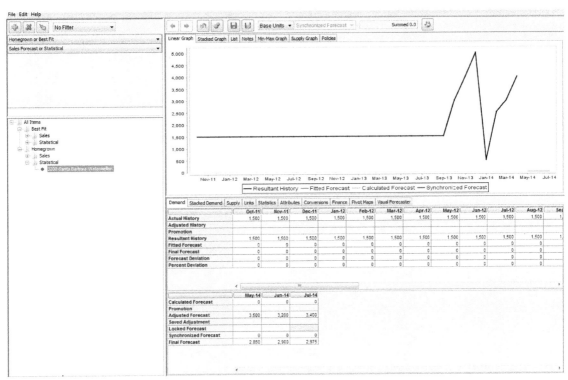

We can do this by uploading the homegrown values to the Adjusted Forecast row. The Calculated forecast (in the lower pane – the history is in the middle pane, and the forecast is in the lower pane). When we save, it saves to the Synchronized Forecast.

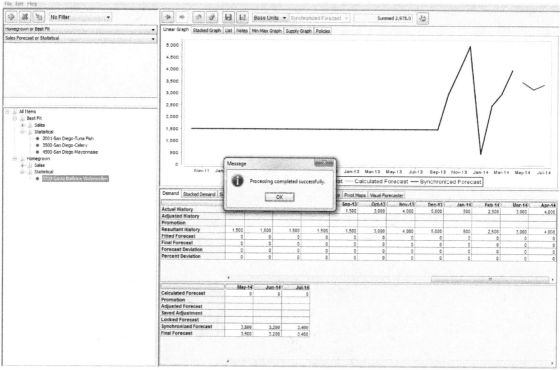

When we finalize the forecast, our imported forecast takes over from any forecast generated within the system. In this way we can carry multiple forecasts within one system — some generated within this system and some generated externally.

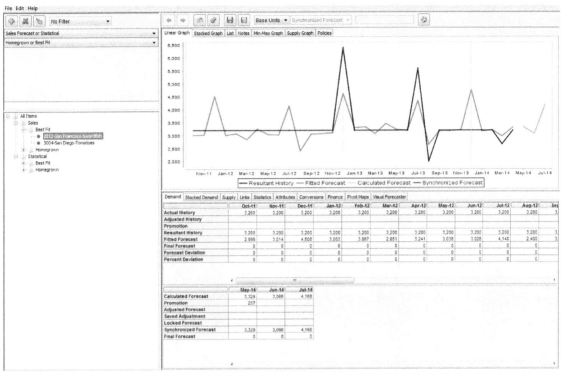

The hierarchy can also be flipped so that the category attributes of Sales or Statistical are higher than those for Best Fit or Homegrown. This is performed in the upper left pane. In this application, any attribute can be placed above or below any other attribute.

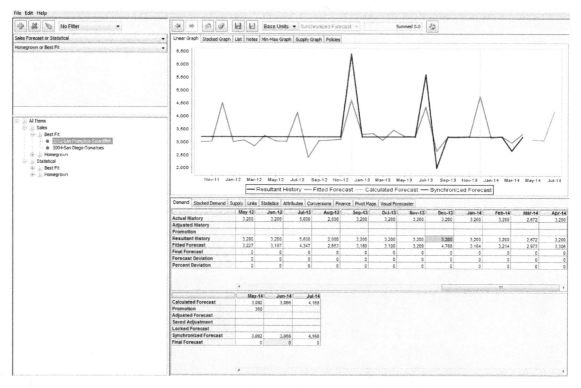

The PLCs under the sales hierarchy are the PLCs for which historically the sales forecast was better than either the best fit or the homegrown forecasting method. However, it is typical to run each statistical forecasting method and to create the initial or
baseline forecast. Then Sales/Marketing provides input, which is used to make adjustments to these forecasts. In this example you can see that the Calculated Forecast,
which was created by the system, is the baseline forecast. However, information from
Sales/Marketing has been used to adjust the forecast. We have one promotion added
and two forecast adjustments. When we save this, all of these changes will be moved to
the Synchronized Forecast row, which is the step before finalizing the forecast.

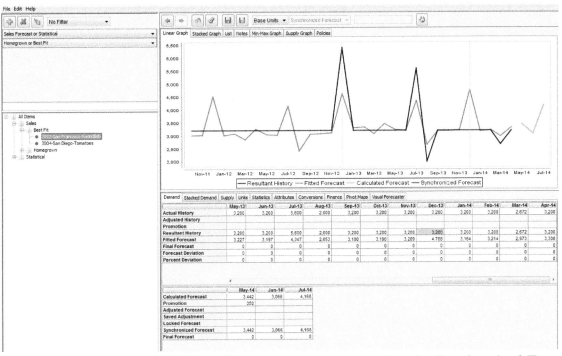

	May-13	Jun-13	Jul-13	Aug-13	Sep-13	Oct-13	Nov-13	Dec-13	Jan-14	Feb-14	Mar-14	Apr-14
Actual History	3,200	3,200	5,600	2,000	3,200	3,200	3,200	3,200	3,200	3,200	2,672	3,200
Adjusted History												
Promotion												
Resultant History	3,200	3,200	5,600	2,000	3,200	3,200	3,200	3,200	3,200	3,200	2,672	3,200
Fitted Forecast	3,227	3,197	4,347	2,653	3,180	3,190	3,209	4,766	3,164	3,214	2,973	3,306
Final Forecast	0	0	0	0	0	0	0	0	0	0	0	0
Forecast Deviation	0	0	0	0	0	0	0	0	0	0	0	0
Percent Deviation	0	0	0	0	0	0	0	0	0	0	0	0

	May-14	Jun-14	Jul-14
Calculated Forecast	3,442	3,066	4,168
Promotion	350		
Adjusted Forecast			
Saved Adjustment			
Locked Forecast			
Synchronized Forecast	3,442	3,066	4,168
Final Forecast	0	0	0

And just as we said, all of these adjustments are now saved to the Synchronized Forecast.

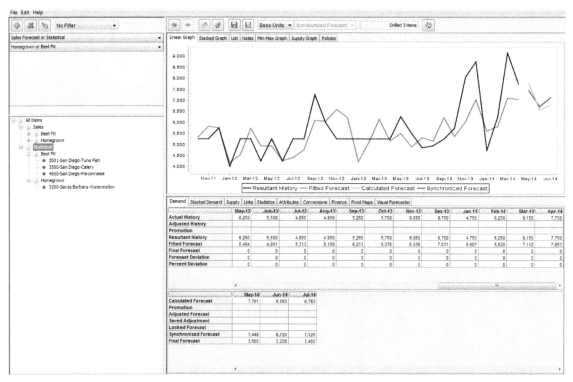

Now if we go and select the Statistical hierarchy node, something that should be re-membered is that the statistical forecast (either best fit or homegrown) beat the sales forecast. Therefore, there is **no reason** to continue to accept Sales input on these PLCs. This helps save time, and helps Sales/Marketing put their limited forecasting time into just those PLCs where they can improve the forecast. The forecasting team will never lose sight of the PLCs for which they required Sales/Marketing input, because they are hard coded right into the attributes of the forecasting system. This application can create many attributes, but normally it is not necessary to show more than a few at a time. This means that this particular hierarchy tree might be hidden much of the time, with another hierarchy tree taking its place.

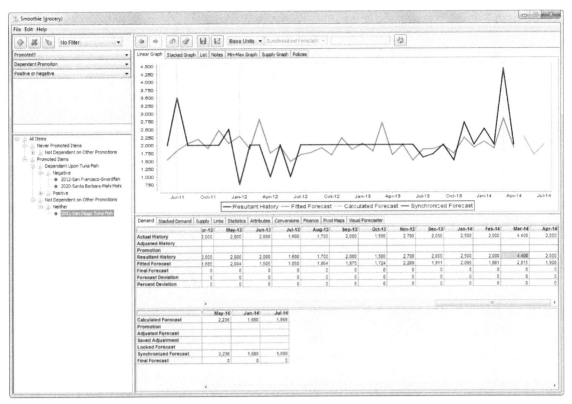

For instance, notice that this hierarchy tree, which I use for managing promotions, is completely different from the hierarchy tree we have been using up to this point. All of these attributes are stored in the same model, but I only show the attributes I need to show at the time.

- *"This structured testing is very important, because too many companies are using guesswork to determine their forecasting strategy. This will not lead to positive outcomes. Once the test is performed, the forecasting strategy can be much more intelligently developed. There are a variety of approaches that can be used, and testing shows when and where each approach should be used. It also allows a strong delineation of who does what. This is one of the most important parts of forecasting, particularly because so many people are often involved in the process.*
- *In order to drive real business results with your sales forecast, the forecast process has to be structured consistently and followed. The key decisions of determining how and when the forecast is captured, who scrubs and vets the forecast, what ongoing analysis is done on the forecast data,*

*and which business decisions are driven from the forecast, need to be
clear at every level and department engaged in the process.*

- *Collaborate internally and externally on the forecast in the interests of
driving the right discussions. This means the focus should often be on the
areas where different forecasters are estimating different results. What is
the reason for those variances? Why do sales and product marketing see
the introduction of a new product so differently?"*

> — 5 Best Practices to Develop a Trusted, Actionable Forecast

These bullet points, directed towards sales forecasting are relevant for both
statistical and sales forecasting.

Who Owns the Forecast?

At many companies there is a debate as to who should "own" the forecast. Here
are some important observations about this question.

- *What Forecast is Being Discussed?:* First of all, there is not one forecast,
  but rather there are **many** forecasts. The sales forecast serves as an
  input to the supply chain forecast, but each entity normally "owns" its
  own forecast. Therefore, when someone asks the question of who owns
  the forecast, it's important to determine what forecast is the topic of the
  conversation.

- *Ownership of the Forecast or Input to the Forecast?:* In many companies
  there is some mixing of terminology between "owning" and "providing
  input to" the forecast. If you **own** something, you are held responsible for
  its outcome. So in the case of forecasting, Sales/Marketing cannot really
  own the supply chain forecast, because they are not held accountable for
  its error. However Sales/Marketing does tend to be held accountable for
  meeting certain forecast dollar targets (Sales much more than Marketing in this regard, although a dollar target has **nothing to do** with the
  PLC forecast). In terms of getting Sales to provide input to the supply
  chain forecast (which is often what people actually mean when they complain that Sales is not properly "owning" the forecast), the best way to
  get Sales/Marketing to provide input is to follow the approach outlined in
  this chapter as it reduces the workload for sales and marketing.

Generally, Sales is not focused on forecast accuracy, particularly at a PLC level. A perfect example of this is the story of the head of Sales who says, *"I don't understand why we stock-out. If you look at the forecast accuracy of sales, it's high! However, we still don't have the right products when the customer demand arrives."* Sales forecast accuracy is typically measured as revenue. Therefore, if Sales forecasts one million dollars in sales, and $900,000 is sold, the forecast is 90 percent accurate. But what does that say about the accuracy of the individual PLC forecast, which is how Supply Chain must measure its forecast accuracy? Absolutely nothing. Therefore, it is well established that while Sales can "own" its sales forecast, the final supply chain forecast is owned by Supply Chain.

Conclusion

This book has focused on the integration of sales and statistical forecasting. It is not enough for a company to be good at either sales or statistical forecasting, or even both sales and statistical forecasting, as it must also be able to combine sales and statistical forecasting. However, the first step in combining the sales and statistical forecast is having a decent quality statistical forecast. If this first step is not achieved, than the orientation becomes around attempting to get a larger proportion of the product location database forecasted by Sales, and this is a recipe for reducing the quality of input from Sales.

The best fit procedure is so important because companies that engage in supply chain management typically have thousands to hundreds of thousands of individual product-location combinations, and in most cases each one of these product-location combinations requires a forecast. This is a lot of line items to keep up with, and a big part of forecast accuracy is choosing the right forecasting model. Best fit forecasting functionality differs greatly by the software applications with the functionality being easy to use in some applications and difficult to use in others. However, the knowledge of how to best leverage best fit forecasting functionality is generally weak in companies, and therefore, most companies don't get anywhere near the benefit that the should from this functionality. Best fit is not the best name for the best fit procedure within most forecasting applications, because forecasting applications do not in fact contain every possible forecasting method that is available. This is demonstrated by the fact that in many cases the best forecasting method is a homegrown approach. In cases where a home grown forecasting method or set of methods has been shown to provide a good forecast accuracy, the home grown method must be compared against the method which is selected by the best fit procedure to select the one best forecasting method per product location combination.

Sales forecasts are well known as biased. This is due to the incentives that are within Sales, which comingle the issue of goal setting with forecasting. As evidence of this, the software vendors Right90 created an application that is primarily focused on quality management of the sales forecast. Sales forecasts often have a bias, which is a consistent forecast error in one direction – either positive or negative. Few authors are willing to see the forecast bias inherent in judgment methods as anything beyond a cognitive bias (that is, an unconscious bias or an error in cognition) and most often companies do not focus on removing forecast bias. This is unfortunate, because once identified, it is relatively easy to adjust forecast bias technically, but often quite different politically. At many companies, Sales/Marketing is considered to have the right domain expertise for forecasting (they understand the products, their customers, and the market). However, their incentives, what these incentives mean for bias, and how this bias might affect the forecast adjustments that they make, are often not accounted for in the management of their input.

One of the biggest myths about sales forecasting is that because Sales has expertise related to market intelligence that they have the tools to convert that market intelligence into the correct adjustments to the forecast. This is not true. Secondly, Sales has its own set of incentives, wants high product availability – is usually less concerned about excess inventory. Within both Sales and Marketing there is a complex set of incentives and motivations that often result in individuals within these groups essentially fighting for capacity, and both groups have incentives to proliferate the product database. Some of these incentives and motivations were illuminated in this book, but they are generally not part of the discourse on how Sales creates forecasts. However, the problem is, no matter if Sales or Marketing were to put an individual measurement emphasis on forecast accuracy, the emphasis would not be sufficient to counteract the effects of forecast bias **of the other** sales measurements. At most companies, the management within Sales and Marketing does not **value** forecast accuracy as highly as they value sales goals.

Another important point to consider is that Sales and Marketing are **not measured** on whether or not they keep inventories low. This is why Sales/Marketing routinely set such unsupportable inventory and service levels. For instance, it is very common for sales groups to target 99 percent service levels for most of its products. However, except for the items with the highest profitability, normally this service level is not sustainable because the inventory rises so dramatically at service levels above 95 percent.

There is an assumption that Sales/Marketing can provide good quality input to the forecast without assistance. Let us analyze that assumption for a moment. Imagine that Sales/Marketing is trained to use the forecasting system. Could a group that has a sales bias, comprised of people with different backgrounds and skill sets than a professional forecaster, outperform a scenario where Sales/Marketing simply provides input to a Forecasting Lead who then creates the forecast? My experience tells me this is highly doubtful. In addition to my anecdotes that lead me to this conclusion, a key observation by those who specialize in managing sales forecasts is that all sales forecasting processes **must** be intermediated.

References

Ailawadi, Kusum L., Karen Gedenk, Christian Lutzky, and Scott A. Neslin, AMA Publishing. *Decomposition of the Sales Impact of Promotion-Induced Stockpiling.* Journal of Marketing Research. August 2007. https://archive.ama.org/Archive/AboutAMA/Pages/AMA%20Publications/AMA%20 Journals/Journal%20of%20Marketing%20Research/TOCs/summary%20aug%2007/ Decompositionjmraug07.aspx.

Armstrong, Scott J., and Fred Collopy. *Integration of Statistical Methods and Judgment for Time Series Forecasting: Principles from Empirical Research.* Forecasting with Judgment. John Wiley and Sons. 1998.

BaseCRM. *Five Reports Every VP of Sales Should Know.* http://resources.getbase.com/5-reports-every-vp-of-sales-should-master-thank-you?-submissionGuid=26f08bab-7b75-49af-8af9-a622c3d8fc15.

BaseCRM. *Understanding Your Pipeline Sales and Tracking.* http://resources.getbase.com/understand-your-pipeline-thank-you?submis-sionGuid=81779455-1fb1-418e-a0a8-8fd01e223416.

Black Box. Accessed June 4, 2014. http://en.wikipedia.org/wiki/Black_box.

Demand Planning and Forecasting.
http://help.sap.com/SCENARIOS_BUS2008/helpdata/EN/49/ed4c6eefc923d3e-
10000000a42189b/content.htm.

Forecasting—Automatic Model Selection using Process 2. November 13, 2008.
http://www.sapfans.com/forums/viewtopic.php?f=6&t=321091.

Goodwin, Paul. *Correct or Combine? Mechanically Integrated Judgment Forecasts
with Statistical Methods.* International Journal of Forecasting. 2000.

Manna, Somnath. *Why to Choose APO over R/3 for Planning.* May 14, 2007.
http://scn.sap.com/thread/406157.

Mello, John E. *Sales Forecast "Game Playing"—Why It's Bad and What You Can Do
About It.* Arkansas University.
http://forecasters.org/foresight/wp/wp-content/uploads/Forecast_Game_Playing_Mel-
lo_OSU_IIF_13.pdf.

Metzer, John, T., and Carol Dienstock. C. *Sales Forecasting Management.* Sage Pub-
lications, 1998.

Right90. *Put the "S" Back into "Sales and Operations" Planning with
Sales Forecasting.*
http://www.right90.com/whitepapers/put_the_s_back_into_sales_and_operations_wp-
FINALPRINT.pdf.

Right90. *Removing Risk From Your Sales Forecast.*
http://www.right90.com/whitepapers/removing_risk_from_your_sales_forecastFI-
NALPRINT.pdf.

Right90. *7 Secrets of Sales Forecasting.*
http://www.right90.com/whitepapers/7_secrets_of_sales_forecastingFINALPRINT.
pdf.

Snapp, Shaun. *A Definition of Forecast Bias.* February 29, 2012.
http://www.scmfocus.com/demandplanning/2012/02/forecastbias/.

Snapp, Shaun. *Forecast Bias Removal with Right90.* September 21, 2010.
http://www.scmfocus.com/demandplanning/2010/09/right90-for-forecast-bias-remov-
al/.

Snapp, Shaun. *How Much Forecast Accuracy Can Be Improved*. February 15, 2012. http://www.scmfocus.com/demandplanning/2012/02/how-much-can-your-forecasting-accuracy-be-improved/.

Snapp, Shaun. *Promotions Forecasting: Techniques of Forecast Adjustments in Software*. SCM Focus Press. 2014.

Snapp, Shaun. *Supply Chain Forecasting Software*. SCM Focus Press. 2012.

Snapp, Shaun. *Why Companies Refuse to Remove Forecast Bias*. July 4, 2010. http://www.scmfocus.com/demandplanning/2010/07/why-do-companies-refuse-to-remove-forecast-bias/.

Stahley, Tim. *From Misery to Mastery: How to Build a Better Sales Forecast*. http://www.right90.com/whitepapers/Misery_to_Mastery_White%20Paper_10_14NO-CHANGES.pdf.

Stockpiling Moms. http://www.stockpilingmoms.com.

Xuanming Su. *Intertemporal Pricing and Consumer Stockpiling*. Operations Research. Vol. 58, No. 4. July-August 2010, pp 1133-1147. http://www.deepdyve.com/lp/informs/intertemporal-pricing-and-consumer-stockpiling-iFZB38Ikz1?articleList=%2Fsearch%3Fquery%3Dstockpiling%2Bpromotions.

Vendor Acknowledgments and Profiles

I have listed brief profiles of each vendor with screen shots included in this book below.

Profiles:

SAP

SAP does not need much of an introduction. They are the largest vendor of enterprise software applications for supply chain management. SAP has multiple products that are showcased in this book, including SAP ERP and SAP APO.

www.sap.com

Demand Works

Demand Works is a best-of-breed demand-and-supply-planning vendor that emphasizes flexible and easy-to-configure solutions. This book only focuses on the supply planning functionality within their Smoothie product, which includes MRP and DRP.

http://www.demandworks.com

Right90

Right90 powers the most accurate forecasts for large complex enterprises from the perspective of sales, regions, finance, shipments over time, product, channel and global accounts. Right90 is very focused on sales forecasting and on bias removal.

http://www.right90.com

BaseCRM

BaseCRM is a leading provider of customer relationship management software.

http://www.basecrm.com

Author Profile

Shaun Snapp is the founder and editor of SCM Focus. SCM Focus is one of the largest independent supply chain software analysis and educational sites on the Internet.

After working at several of the largest consulting companies and at i2 Technologies, he became an independent consultant and later started SCM Focus. He maintains a strong interest in comparative software design, and works both in SAP APO as well as with a variety of best-of-breed supply chain planning vendors. His ongoing relationships with these vendors keep him on the cutting edge of emerging technology.

Primary Sources of Information and Writing Topics

Shaun writes about topics with which he has firsthand experience. These topics range from recovering problematic implementations, to system configuration, to socializing complex software and supply chain concepts in the areas of demand planning, supply planning and production planning.

More broadly, he writes on topics supportive of these applications, which include master data parameter management, integration, analytics, simulation and bill of material management systems. He covers management aspects of enterprise software ranging from software policy to handling consulting partners on SAP projects.

Shaun writes from an implementer's perspective and as a result he focuses on how software is actually used in practice rather than its hypothetical or "pure release note capabilities." Unlike many authors in enterprise software who keep their distance from discussing the realities of software implementation, he writes both on the problems as well as the successes of his software use. This gives him a distinctive voice in the field.

Secondary Sources of Information

In addition to project experience, Shaun's interest in academic literature is a secondary source of information for his books and articles. Intrigued with the historical perspective of supply chain software, much of his writing is influenced by his readings and research into how different categories of supply chain software developed, evolved, and finally became broadly used over time.

Covering the Latest Software Developments

Shaun is focused on supply chain software selections and implementation improvement through writing and consulting, bringing companies some of the newest technologies and methods. Some of the software developments that Shaun showcases at SCM Focus and in books at SCM Focus Press have yet to reach widespread adoption.

Education

Shaun has an undergraduate degree in business from the University of Hawaii, a Master of Science in Maritime Management from the Maine Maritime Academy and a Master of Science in Business Logistics from Penn State University. He has taught both logistics and SAP software.

Software Certifications

Shaun has been trained and/or certified in products from i2 Technologies, Servigistics, ToolsGroup and SAP (SD, DP, SNP, SPP, EWM).

Contact

Shaun can be contacted at:
shaunsnapp@scmfocus.com

Abbreviations

CRM – Customer Relationship Management

ERP – Enterprise Resource Planning

MAPE – Mean Absolute Percent Error

PLC – Product Location Combination

RMSE – Root Mean Square Error

SCM – Supply Chain Management

SKU – Stock Keeping Unit

Links Listed in the Book by Chapter

Chapter 1:

http://www.scmfocus.com/writing-rules/

http://www.scmfocus.com

http://www.scmfocus.com/scmfocuspress/sales-and-statistical-forecast-ing-combined/

Chapter 3:

http://www.scmfocus.com/demandplanning/2010/09/why-companies-are-selecting-the-wrong-supply-chain-demand-planning-systems/ [1]

http://www.scmfocus.com/3S/

---

[1] I cover this in more detail in the SCM Focus Press book *Supply Chain Forecasting Software.*

Chapter 6:

http://www.scmfocus.com/demandplanning/2012/02/how-much-can-your-forecasting-accuracy-be-improved/

http://www.scmfocus.com/demandplanning/2012/02/forecastbias/

http://www.scmfocus.com/demandplanning/2010/07/why-do-companies-refuse-to-remove-forecast-bias/

http://www.scmfocus.com/3s/

http://forecasters.org/foresight/wp/wp-content/uploads/Forecast_Game_Playing_Mello_OSU_IIF_13.pdf

Chapter 8:

http://en.wikipedia.org/wiki/Meta-analysis

www.ingramcontent.com/pod-product-compliance
Lightning Source LLC
LaVergne TN
LVHW080100070326
832902LV00014B/2338